Theological and Scientific Commentary on Darwin's *Origin of Species*

Theological and Scientific Commentary on Darwin's *Origin of Species*

Ted Peters
Martinez Hewlett

Abingdon Press
Nashville

This book is printed on acid-free paper.

Library of Congress Cataloging-in-Publication Data

Peters, Ted, 1941–
    Theological and scientific commentary on Darwin's Origin of species / Ted Peters and Martinez Hewlett.
        p. cm.
    Includes bibliographical references (p.   ).
    ISBN: 978-0-687-64939-6 (binding: adhesive, pbk. with ce insert : alk. paper)
    1. Darwin, Charles, 1908–1882. On the origin of species.   2. Evolution (Biology)—Religious aspects—Christianity.   3. Religion and science.   I. Hewlett, Martinez J. (Martinez Joseph), 1942– III. Title.

QH365.O8P48   2008
576.8'2—dc22

                                                                                            2008010327

Excerpts from and digital version of Darwin's *Origin of Species* reproduced with permission from *The Complete Works of Charles Darwin Online,* John van Wyhe ed. (http://darwin-online.org.uk/).

08 09 10 11 12 13 14 15 16 17—10 9 8 7 6 5 4 3 2 1

MANUFACTURED IN THE UNITED STATES OF AMERICA

CONTENTS

1360

TABLE OF ILLUSTRATIONS

PREFACE

Nearly fourteen billion years have passed since the Big Bang. More than four billion years have elapsed since planet Earth cooled and began its cyclic orbit of our sun. We estimate that about three billion years have passed since the first cellular life forms established a tenuous foothold in the nutrient-rich primordial sea. About 1.5 billion years ago our eukaryotic ancestors radiated throughout the ecological niches of the biosphere. Three and a half million years in our past our prehuman primate ancestors stood upright to see farther across the ancient savannahs of their home. Measured against such a scale of deep time, the two hundred years since the birth of Charles Darwin and the 150 years since the publication of *On the Origin of Species by Means of Natural Selection* seem trivial indeed. And yet, it is fair to say that few other publications within this short span of our recent history have even approached the level of impact this one book has had on the way we see ourselves as human beings in the wider world of nature.

The impact of this one book, hereinafter referred to as *Origin*, defined the concept of evolution precisely as the development of new species over deep time through the action of natural selection on variations in inheritance. This insight regarding the decisive role of natural selection has set the paradigm for modern biology, a principle that no research scientist today can ignore. Darwin's theory has proved itself to be fertile for the growth of new knowledge, not only in retrieving our biological heritage but also in predicting what researchers in genetics can expect to find.

Darwin's book of science has also become a book of religion. We might go further to say that no other book penned by a scientist has elicited such a strong reaction in the history of religion. Like Mount Vesuvius erupting, the fallout from *Origin's* explosion is still raining down upon us. On the one hand, a significant minority of conservative Christians have worried and still worry that if Darwin is right—that speciation is solely the result of natural selection—then God's purposeful action will have been removed from the natural world. Darwin himself, worrying about the theological implications of his theory, wondered if he might have become the "Devil's Chaplain." On the other hand, many Christians of a more liberal stripe who yearn for reconciliation between science and faith are looking for ways to integrate Darwin and Christian belief. The majority of Christian believers have made their peace with the evolutionary worldview, even if they harbor some belief that the soul of human beings renders us distinguishable from the rest of God's creatures. Jewish theologians have for the most part absorbed the Darwinian worldview without conflict; while Muslim intellectuals are nearly as divided as the Christians. Unwittingly, *Origin* has come to mark the divide between contestants in our religious struggles.

The year 2009 marks two anniversaries. The first is the 200th birthday of Charles Darwin, born February 12, 1809. The second is the 150th anniversary of the publication of Darwin's *On the Origin of Species by Natural Selection*, actually on November 22 of that year. Because of the interaction between Darwin and his reading audience, he revised this seminal work numerous times. We offer here the sixth and final edition, one that includes Darwin's own answer to his late nineteenth-century critics. This anniversary year provides the right moment for a scientist and a theologian to pause and ask together: just where are we in the history of science and religion regarding the question of evolution?

As of this writing we are still a rather unique team examining issues dealing with evolution and religion—actually, *theology* as reflection upon religion, as we prefer to call our approach. There are both scientists and theologians of note who have and who still engage these topics. However, we seem to stand apart as a closely knit working pair of scientist and theologian. Ted Peters is professor of systematic theology at Pacific Lutheran Theological Seminary at the Graduate Theological Union (GTU) in Berkeley, California. Martinez Hewlett is professor emeritus of molecular and cellular biology at the University of Arizona in Tucson, and he also serves as adjunct professor for the Dominican School of Philosophy and Theology at the GTU. Both of us are affiliated with the Center for Theology and the Natural Sciences at the GTU.

Ted writes on various topics in theology. He has also written extensively on bioethical issues surrounding genetics. He continues in this vein with both books and articles as well as work on various advisory boards, including at this writing the Scientific and Medical Accountability Standards working group of the California Institute for Regenerative Medicine. Marty Hewlett has had a career as a molecular virologist and is the coauthor of one of the major textbooks in that field. In recent years he has turned his attention to philosophy of science.

Some time ago, we, Ted and Marty, came together to study the biological role in evolution of violence, suffering, death, genocide, and extinction. Our concern was to evaluate the claim made by some theistic evolutionists that God has employed our evolutionary history to bring the human race into existence. If this is the case, we thought we would need to investigate the place of a nature "red in tooth and claw," to borrow the phrase from Alfred Lord Tennyson, in God's creative work. The question of the place of evil in nature brought us together as research partners. This has been and remains our research concern.

However, our work has led us on what at first looked like a detour; we began to investigate the puzzling if not confusing public controversy regarding the scientific veracity of evolutionary theory and its religious implications. This is the battle between laboratory scientists, schoolteachers, materialists, atheists, creationists, intelligent design advocates, and theistic evolutionists. How do all of these fit together? This became our question. Assuming we should come to understand empathetically what each party in the argument believes from his or her point of view, we visited and interviewed advocates for various positions. We pondered all the pieces of the puzzle before trying to put them together. Our attempt to put together this puzzle has been going on for more than a decade now.

Our process, from a team perspective, has been to drill beneath the contemporary controversy as well as drill beneath the late nineteenth-century controversy to get to the underlying science. It has appeared to us that the Darwinian model of evolution is fertile science; yet this treasure lies buried beneath layers and layers of ideology, social programs, religious commitments, and moral rhetoric. Once having drilled beneath the ideologies, we explored the various ways in which Darwinian science itself represents the best explanatory and most fruitful model to describe, using natural laws, how the diversity of life that we observe arose.

After satisfying ourselves that Darwin's model represents the best science, we returned upward to examine the layers of philosophical, religious, and societal understandings based on the concept of evolution that have made their way into the popular consciousness. We have followed ideological trails from the late nineteenth century to our present era. We have traced the agnosticism and atheism represented by Darwin's friend and contemporary Thomas Huxley to the present-day evolutionary biologist, Richard Dawkins. We followed the social Darwinists and theorists, from Herbert Spencer and Francis Galton to the sociobiologists and evolutionary psychologists of today. And we have charted objectors to this theory, including the scientific creationists and the intelligent design theorists.

Have we ourselves taken a stand? Yes, we have. Our own piece in this puzzling array of alternative positions we call *theistic evolution*. We are by no means the first to hold such a position or to use such a label. Many Christian thinkers before us have combined the scientific concept of evolution with the Christian concept of creation to develop a worldview that includes progress in both biology and society. We do not accept the doctrine of progress; yet we have taken out membership in the club of theistic evolutionists. At a minimum, we hold that belief in God and the science of biological evolution are not mutually exclusive. We avow that one does not have to accept the ideological positions of atheism or scientism or materialism to be an evolutionary biologist; and we would like the science that the theologian takes seriously to be Darwin's model of evolution.

Beyond the minimum, we affirm that God's plan for both creation and redemption include the long history of life's development and the arrival at this stage of the human race. Rather than see a principle of future progress within nature, we rely upon God's promise of a transformation of nature. In our version of theistic evolution, we combine our inherited nature "red in tooth and claw" with God's promise in Isaiah that the lion will lie down with the lamb (Isa 11:6-9). God has a purpose *for* nature even if we cannot now discern purpose *in* nature. We have elaborated this position in two coauthored books.[1]

It is not our purpose in this celebratory volume to further defend our own position. Rather, we wish to provide the kind of introduction to the thought of Charles Darwin that can link the original text of *Origin* to the contemporary laboratory and pew. We intend to lead you on an exploration of the scientific and theological as well as the societal developments that took place leading up to Darwin's work, the work itself, the time since its publication to the present, and to give you a peek at what the future might be. We will do this from our perspectives as scientist, as theologian, and together as theistic evolutionists.

This means that in our journey together in this introduction we will leave you with some take-home messages that will be repeated in one form or another. They are:

1. Today's evolutionary biology, inspired as it is by Charles Darwin's insight, is the best available explanatory model for how the diversity of life forms arose. Combined now with new knowledge in genetics, the synthesis of genetic variation and natural selection provides the most fruitful model for guiding laboratory research toward new and important areas of scientific exploration.
2. The philosophical and societal overlays of atheism, social Darwinism, eugenics, and materialism were added after the fact of the science. That is, the data leading to the development of Darwin's model do not require an acceptance of any of these ideologies in order for the model to work at the level of science.
3. A belief in God is not antithetical to the science of evolutionary biology. In fact, many theologians fully embrace biological evolution in their consideration of how God's actions in creation are expressed. And, at the same time, many scientists are not only believers, but see their faith strengthened by the wonders they observe in the natural world. The Bible is a book that communicates how God redeems, whereas nature provides a book that communicates something about how God creates. Science helps us interpret that second book.

In chapter 1 ("*Origin of Species:* The Science of Darwinian Evolution") we look at exactly what data Charles Darwin used and what he concluded. In doing this, we quote from the text itself and provide you with references to this material on the accompanying CD of the book. It is here that we make the case for this being a truly remarkable scientific development with far-reaching implications. In chapter 2 ("Drilling through the Layers of Ideology") we follow the fate of the science as it is buried or wrapped up in the ideological layers of atheism, materialism, social Darwinism, eugenics, and progress. In chapter 3 ("The Many Theologies of Evolution") we examine the array of the religious responses, both positive and negative, that have taken place since publication of the book. In chapter 4 ("Scientific Concepts: Then and Now") we have selected seven key concepts that were important in Darwin's formulation of his model, and how these concepts have changed over the 150 years since publication. In chapter 5 ("Design in Biology: What Darwin Could and Could Not See") we pay special attention to the issue of design, particularly because of the contemporary discussion surrounding so-called intelligent design. In chapter 6 ("What Does It Mean to Be Human?") we bring the commentary to a close with the question of how the evolutionary model affects our view of who we are. We end with an annotated bibliography for further exploration.

For those of our readers who are students in the sciences, we hope that this journey with us will enrich your understanding of the place evolutionary biology holds as one of the seminal developments of our age. We also want you to take away a sense of how the arguments about this science are really not about the science at all, but about ideology that has been overlaid on it. For our readers who are students in the humanities or social sciences, we hope that our comments on the way in which Darwin used observational science to construct the best explanatory model using natural principles will give you a clearer understanding of why evolutionary biology is science and not philosophy or theology.

We hope that all of our readers, students and professors, cleric and lay, believers and nonbelievers, will come away with an appreciation of how important it is for Christians to champion the best science and the best theological reflection on that science. We send you on your way through our chapters with one of our favorite and oft-repeated quotes from a distinguished theistic evolutionist, Pope John Paul II:

> Science can purify religion from error and superstition; religion can purify science from idolatry and false absolutes. Each can draw the other into a wider world, a world in which both can flourish.[2]

ORIGIN OF SPECIES: THE SCIENCE OF DARWINIAN EVOLUTION

N ot a day goes by in biological science that, either explicitly or implicitly, the Darwinian model of descent with modification through natural selection is not invoked. It is to the credit of this powerful theory that we continually accumulate supporting evidence for its basic principles, while at the same time using it to generate new and fruitful lines of investigation. Despite its value to science, however, social upheaval over the religious and ethical implications of Charles Darwin's theory continue to foment cultural and even political turmoil. As we commemorate the 200th anniversary of Charles Darwin's birth and the 150th anniversary of his publication of *On the Origin of Species by Natural Selection*, the impact of both the scientific value and the religious viewpoint of Darwin's theory is more apparent than ever.

Here we will turn first to the science. In later chapters we will give attention to the religious ferment.

THE SCIENTIFIC SETTING OF *ORIGIN*

It is fun to imagine what it must have been like that day in late November of 1859 when publisher John Murray released the long-anticipated text of *Origin* from his publishing company on Albemarle Street in the Mayfair district of London. Murray had been persuaded by Charles Lyell, the eminent geologist, to accept this manuscript from Darwin, having examined the first three chapters in April of 1859. Of the initial 1,250 copy print run, about 1,200 copies made it into general circulation, the balance being distributed to the author, to reviewers, and to the copyright office. Within days of its release, it is likely that most, if not all, of the copies were sold, at about fifteen shillings each. It is unlikely that this book release in any way matched the sales of a modern book event, such as the recent final book of the Harry Potter series. Nonetheless, this thoroughly scientific text would eventually see six editions, all under the editorial supervision of Darwin himself; and it would change the way that biologists in particular and everyone in general views the natural living world.

What exactly was Darwin's contribution to the world of science? Was he the lone revolutionary thinker whose theory challenged the rest of the establishment? Not exactly. The idea that species of living things were not fixed but likely derived from earlier forms had been proposed and discussed by some physical scientists and naturalists, including his promoter Charles Lyell. Evolution was in the cultural air, so to speak. Although the majority of scientists had not yet embraced this nascent evolutionary view, the scientific innovators were becoming noticed. Darwin noticed them, as he states in the preface to the sixth edition of *Origin*:

> Until recently the great majority of naturalists believed that species were immutable productions, and had been separately created. This view has been ably maintained by many authors. Some few naturalists, on the other hand, have believed that species undergo modification, and that the existing forms of life are the descendants by true generation of pre-existing forms.[1]

No, Darwin himself did not invent the concept of evolution. Darwin's great achievement was to synthesize these previous ideas, derive, as a hypothesis, a naturalistic explanation for them, and present a wealth of observational data to support his hypothesis. In this sense, he was much like a modern scientist, working from his own perspective while crediting the ideas of his predecessors. However, he was clearly at the fringe of his discipline, since, as he states above, most biologists ("naturalists") would have thought that species were unchanging ("immutable") and had been created in the form in which we see them. In modern terms, he was pushing the edge of the envelope.

He also presented these ideas in a cogent, well-supported argument. Over the course of the six editions, he took great pains to answer his scientific critics, adding to each edition his counters to their positions. In addition, his work met with the support of some of the most influential thinkers of his time, including Lyell, Thomas Huxley, Francis Galton, Asa

Gray, and Herbert Spencer. All of this ensured that the book would not only be taken seriously but also be widely read in the scientific community.

What was the state of biology, as we now call the discipline, when the young naturalist Charles Darwin walked onto H.M.S. *Beagle* in December 1831 to begin a nearly five-year adventure? Certainly, like any science, it was observational. However, it had no theoretical foundation and, as a science yet to mature, was in its infancy.

Carolus Linnaeus had, in the early eighteenth century, established the system of classification that, with subsequent modifications over the years, is still the standard. With this in hand, it had become possible for a naturalist to have a reasonably sophisticated descriptive framework of the living world. And so it was that a ship's naturalist such as Darwin set out to observe the biota he would encounter with an understanding of these species relationships.

Of course, at the time of his voyage most naturalists assumed that all extant species of plants and animals had been separately created in the form in which we observe them. This had been Linnaeus's presupposition in his great work, *Systema Naturae*. It was not just a church-imposed doctrine, since it seemed to be consistent with the present state of information about the living world.

By the time the *Beagle* left on her round-the-world trip, however, there were accumulations of observations that were undermining the idea of species fixed by God at creation's beginning. For instance, it was becoming clear that the earth is much older than the Genesis account would indicate. Rather than being thousands of years old, geologists were beginning to understand Earth's age in millions of years, if not more. Our modern calculation of 4.5 billion years, based in part on radiometric determinations, was not available; but scientists of the nineteenth century were convinced that the age of the earth was on the order of one to four hundred million years old. More important, however, Charles Lyell introduced the idea that the planet had undergone a constant and gradual rate of change over this time, a position called by William Whewell "uniformitarianism." This had great influence on Darwin's ideas. He read the first volume of Lyell's book, *Principles of Geology*, at the beginning of his voyage on the *Beagle*:

> I had brought with me the first volume of Lyell's *Principles of Geology*, which I studied attentively; and this book was of the highest service to me in many ways. The very first place which I examined, namely St. Jago in the Cape Verde islands, showed me clearly the wonderful

superiority of Lyell's manner of treating geology, compared with that of any other author, whose works I had with me or ever afterwards read.[2]

In fact, so important is the work of Lyell for Darwin that, at one point in *Origin*, he admonishes his reader against any criticism of its conclusions:

> He who can read Sir Charles Lyell's grand work on the *Principles of Geology*, which the future historian will recognise as having produced a revolution in natural science, and yet does not admit how vast have been the past periods of time, may at once close this volume.[3]

A second major influence on Darwin's thinking was the work of Robert Thomas Malthus. In his influential book, *An Essay on the Principle of Population*, published in 1798, Malthus proposed that populations, which increase geometrically, would inevitably outstrip resources, which increase arithmetically. Darwin concluded from this that there would be a struggle for reproduction and existence, which only the most suited could win. He says:

> A struggle for existence inevitably follows from the high rate at which all organic beings tend to increase. Every being, which during its natural life-time produces several eggs or seeds, must suffer destruction during some period of its life, and during some season or occasional year, otherwise, on the principle of geometrical increase, its numbers would quickly become so inordinately great that no country could support the product. Hence, as more individuals are produced than can possibly survive, there must in every case be a struggle for existence, either one individual with another of the same species, or with the individuals of distinct species, or with the physical conditions of life. It is the doctrine of Malthus applied with manifold force to the whole animal and vegetable kingdoms; for in this case there can be no artificial increase of food, and no prudential restraint from marriage. Although some species may be now increasing, more or less rapidly, in numbers, all cannot do so, for the world would not hold them.[4]

Another feature of early nineteenth-century science was the great fascination with fossil forms, many of which were discovered as geologists, paleontologists, and naturalists explored the world. The identification and classification of fossil remains had become a central feature of the uniformitarian view of the planet, given that the age of such remains could be correlated with the strata in which they were deposited. Darwin himself had unearthed fossil remains, especially during his *Beagle* voyage. In Argentina, he found examples of now-extinct mammals, including an ancestral horse:

> When I found in La Plata the tooth of a horse embedded with the remains of Mastodon, Megatherium, Toxodon and other extinct monsters, which all co-existed with still living shells at a very late geological period, I was filled with astonishment.[5]

Darwin was not trained as a paleontologist and, when he returned to England, the fossil records of his discoveries, which he edited, were analyzed by Richard Owen, a distinguished London expert in vertebrates. The publication of these observations comprised nineteen reports, released between 1838 and 1843, all supervised by Darwin, and prepared by one of several London experts.

THE DARWINIAN MODEL

And so it was, armed with Lyell's uniformitarian view of the history of the earth, the record of both fossils and living plants and animals from his voyage and the work of others, and the population theories of Malthus, Darwin set out to formulate an explanatory model for how the observed species might have arisen. He based his model by analogy on the practical methods that breeders had used for centuries in selecting for desired traits in livestock or crops. In contrast to this artificial selection, he proposed a role for what he named, and what we still call, *natural selection*.

Darwin proposed that all currently existing species, a term he was careful to define and that we will cover in more detail below, had descended from ancestral types over long geological periods of time. This descent occurred by the accumulation of slight variations in individuals, which variations were inherited by their offspring. With limited resources and large populations competing for those resources, only individuals whose traits gave them an advantage would survive and reproduce, passing those traits on. Thus, the individuals, and therefore the population, would be subject to a selection:

> All these results . . . follow from the struggle for life. Owing to this struggle, variations, however slight and from whatever cause proceeding, if they be in any degree profitable to the individuals of a species, in their

infinitely complex relations to other organic beings and to their physical conditions of life, will tend to the preservation of such individuals, and will generally be inherited by the offspring. The offspring, also, will thus have a better chance of surviving, for, of the many individuals of any species which are periodically born, but a small number can survive. I have called this principle, by which each slight variation, if useful, is preserved, by the term natural selection, in order to mark its relation to man's power of selection.[6]

One consequence of this model is that ancestral forms that contained traits that did not increase their likelihood of survival would have ceased to be represented and would thus be extinct. The record of these ancestral forms would therefore only be present as fossils, where such remnants could be preserved. As we shall see, the incompleteness of the fossil record was an objection that plagued Darwin himself and continues to be raised by dissenters to this day.

A key component of Darwin's model is the necessity that the reproduction of organisms leads to offspring that have traits very much like their parents. This process, called *inheritance*, is essential if traits that ensure the survival of the population are to be passed on to subsequent generations. But exactly how did this work? At the time of the publication of *Origin*, very little was known about the laws governing inheritance, as Darwin clearly states:

> The laws governing inheritance are for the most part unknown; no one can say why the same peculiarity in different individuals of the same species, or in different species, is sometimes inherited and sometimes not so; why the child often reverts in certain characteristics to its grandfather or grandmother or more remote ancestor; why a peculiarity is often transmitted from one sex to both sexes, or to one sex alone, more commonly but not exclusively to the like sex.[7]

Now, history works in random yet interesting ways. The above passage is taken from the definitive sixth edition, published in 1872. This is after considerable editorial changes by Darwin, in light of new information and in answer to criticisms. Note the date. By this time, a lengthy paper had appeared in the *Proceedings of the Brün Society for Natural Science*, written by Gregor Mendel and describing his quantitative results from experiments with pea hybrids. These results form the basis for understanding the nature of inheritance. It is clear that Mendel's genetics, as it has come to be called, was presented to a scientific community that was not ready to understand it. Included in this would have been Charles Darwin.

The nature of inheritance was of critical importance to Darwin, as we can see from the amount of effort he devotes in *Origin* to discussing what he then knew about the subject. Darwin, like virtually all naturalists in the late nineteenth century, subscribed to the idea that traits of parents were blended in their offspring. Blending inheritance would be the norm, with certain notable exceptions that continued to be observed. Darwin was convinced of this model of inheritance.[8] As we will see, this conviction would come to haunt Darwin in defending the model; but he would ultimately be rescued by the rediscovery of Mendel's genetics. Mendel's genetics could explain the variations in inheritance that Darwin had observed. Mendel's genetics would eventually be adopted into Darwin's evolutionary scheme, forming the neo-Darwinian synthesis. Natural selection acts on inherited variation, selecting some traits for survival while leaving others to extinction.

Variations in inheritance are essential to Darwin's version of evolution. It is the inherited individual differences upon which natural selection could act:

> These individual differences are of the highest importance for us, for they are often inherited, as must be familiar to every one; and they thus afford materials for natural selection to act on and accumulate, in the same manner as man accumulates in any given direction individual differences in his domesticated productions.[9]

Darwin was methodologically prescient. Something had to account for inherited differences. Blending? Something else? Eventually the discovery of genetic mutations would provide an explanation for the slight variations in inheritance upon which natural selection would do its work.

PUBLICATION OF SUBSEQUENT EDITIONS AND RESPONSES TO CRITICISMS

Darwin was already revising his text as the first edition was being released. In some sense, this first edition was a draft, given that he was rushed in its production by the impetus of Alfred Wallace's work. Darwin and Wallace presented joint papers before the Linnaen Society, subsequently published in their proceedings in 1858. Darwin was thus under considerable pressure to produce his work quickly. His immediate editing likely stems from his consideration of this first publication as only an abstract of his ideas.

The second edition, appearing only a few months after the first, had a few minor changes, including additional epigrams (see discussion of epigrams below). Editions three through five increasingly added to the revisions that Darwin would make, with the fifth edition finally including the phrase "survival of the fittest," coined by Herbert Spencer. Darwin substitutes this expression for natural selection and struggle for survival:

> But the expression often used by Mr. Herbert Spencer, of the Survival of the Fittest, is more accurate, and is sometimes equally convenient.[10]

The sixth and final edition of *Origin* appeared in 1872 and contains all of the revisions that Darwin had made, along with an extensive response to scientific criticisms that had been either published or mentioned to him and that he took seriously enough to mount a reply.

There are a few things worth noting in the case of these revisions. First, Darwin introduced the *Historical Sketch*, in which he summarizes all of the work leading up to the publication of his first edition. After mentioning that Aristotle had some "foreshadowing" of natural selection in his physics, he begins with mentioning the work of Georges-Louis Leclerc (Comte de Buffon) in the late eighteenth century and concludes with 1859 publications by Thomas Huxley and John Hooker.

Second, Darwin devotes two full chapters in the sixth edition (chapter 6: "Difficulties of the Theory"; chapter 7: "Miscellaneous Objections to the Theory"), along with a portion of a later chapter (chapter 10: "On the Imperfection of the Geological Record") to answer his own critiques and, more important, the criticisms of others. Two of the difficulties are subsequently addressed in their own chapters: the problem of instinct (chapter 8) and the issue of hybrids (chapter 9). At the beginning of chapter 6, Darwin catalogues what he calls "a crowd of difficulties" with the theory. Most, if not all, of these difficulties are still with us today. It appears to us that modern critics in both the creationist and intelligent design camps have not come up with anything that Darwin had not anticipated.

First, the issue of the rarity of transitional forms is mentioned:

> why, if species have descended from other species by fine gradations, do we not everywhere see innumerable transitional forms? Why is not all nature in confusion, instead of the species being, as we see them, well defined?[11]

Second, the problems that haunt the debate with the creationists (the issue of how speciation can take place) and fuel the intelligent design program (the question of how complex structures can be the product of natural selection):

> is it possible that an animal having, for instance, the structure and habits of a bat, could have been formed by the modification of some other animal with widely different habits and structure? Can we believe that natural selection could produce, on the one hand, an organ of trifling importance, such as the tail of a giraffe, which serves as a fly-flapper, and, on the other hand, an organ so wonderful as the eye?[12]

Third, the concern about how instincts can be subject to natural selection:

> Can instincts be acquired and modified through natural selection? What shall we say to the instinct which leads the bee to make cells, and which has practically anticipated the discoveries of profound mathematicians?[13]

Fourth, the central issue of the reproductive isolation of species, contrasted with the ability of varieties within species to produce offspring:

> How can we account for species, when crossed, being sterile and producing sterile offspring, whereas, when varieties are crossed, their fertility is unimpaired?[14]

Darwin answers the first class of objections by addressing the obvious imperfection of the fossil record (detailed in chapter 10) and by asserting that successful variations (varieties) will, by competition, eliminate the previous unsuccessful versions of the same organism. Thus, the rarity of transitional forms in the present day is a result of natural selection in action.

The second class of problems is of particular interest. In chapter 7 Darwin addresses what he calls "miscellaneous objections." However, most of this chapter is devoted to a detailed response to a book published in 1871 by the zoologist, St. George Mivart, entitled *The Genesis of Species*.[15] In this work, Mivart details a number of objections, not to evolution per se, but to natural selection as the driving force for the process. His objections constitute an interesting set of statements that will be echoed more than one hundred years later in the positions of the intelligent design (ID) movement.

Mivart was concerned that natural selection, by acting gradually over long periods of time, could not account for preserving changes that would ultimately result in useful or selectable traits. For instance, he wondered how the beginning stages of the elongation of the giraffe's neck could have any selective advantage with respect to the ultimate result, that of getting food from higher reaches of plants or (more likely) being able to detect the approach of predators sooner.

Mivart's explanation was that, rather than the external force of natural selection, there was some "internal" force that propelled the variation into a particular direction. This force would be of some unknown kind but would be explainable by natural laws. It is interesting to read this with "irreducible complexity" or "specified complexity," the watchwords of the ID movement, in mind. We will deal specifically with ID in a later chapter of this introductory analysis.

Darwin addresses each of Mivart's examples in turn, dealing with them by citing specific counterexamples of gradual variation that results, in Darwin's opinion, in selection. All along he appeals to natural selection as a condition of the environment in which species find themselves, rather than asserting some internal force of directed variation. Most of Darwin's arguments effectively refute the objections raised by Mivart, although it must be noted that his claim for the gradual evolution of the giraffe in spite of the objection that the larger size would have meant the need for more food is, in fact, what Stephen Jay Gould would have called a "just so story." Darwin argues:

> To this conclusion Mr. Mivart brings forward two objections. One is that the increased size of the body would obviously require an increased supply of food, and he considers it as "very problematical whether the disadvantages thence arising would not, in times of scarcity, more than counterbalance the advantages." But as the giraffe does actually exist in large numbers in Africa, and as some of the largest antelopes in the world, taller than an ox, abound there, why should we doubt that, as far as size is concerned, intermediate gradations could formerly have existed there, subjected as now to severe dearths. Assuredly the being able to reach, at each stage of increased size, to a supply of food, left untouched by the other hoofed quadrupeds of the country, would have been of some advantage to the nascent giraffe.[16]

Darwin's discussion of the inheritance and selection of instinctive behavior is quite important, given the suggestions of the late twentieth-century field we know as *evolutionary psychology*. Clearly, Darwin's arguments here must differ, since behavior is not the same as organic structure. Transitional forms of behavior cannot leave a physical fossil record, but must be inferred from presently living examples. As a result, much of Darwin's argument rests on his use of artificial selection during purposeful breeding as a sound analogy for natural selection. If we can select for dogs, such as Marty's chocolate Labrador retriever Molly, who have instincts useful for hunting, then certainly in nature such instinctive behaviors can be subject to selection. With this as a prelude, Darwin then describes a host of very specific examples of such instinctive behavior. At this stage in the development of the theory, Darwin has no objective proof for his assertions. As we shall see in a later chapter, the attempt to document this is the province of sociobiology and its derivative disciplines.

As already mentioned, perhaps the most telling scientific objection to Darwin's theory stemmed from his inability in his own era to offer a cogent working understanding of inheritance. This was not, of course, his fault. As we noted earlier, Darwin, as a naturalist of his day, thought that the process of reproduction led to a blending of the traits of the parents in the offspring. He discussed this as early as his 1842 and 1844 essays sketching the general features of his theory.[17] In fact, he already recognized at this time a significant problem: if traits are blended in offspring, how could an advantageous development not be swamped out by this process?

Fleeming Jenkin, a professor of engineering at University College in London, published in 1867 a review of *Origin* in *The North British Review*.[18] Vorzimmer categorizes Jenkin's critique into two categories: first, a limit on the range or scope of possible variations leading to selectable differences, and second, that major variations from the normal form (saltations or "sports") were rare and, more importantly, would be swamped out by blending with normal traits during the process of reproduction.[19] To quote from Jenkin:

> To put this case clearly beside the former, we may say that if in a tribe of a given number of individuals there appears one super-eminently gifted, and if the advantage accruing to the descendants bears some kind of proportion to the amount of the ancestor's blood in their veins, the chances are considerable that for the first few generations he will have many descendants; but by degrees this advantage wanes, and after many generations the chances are so far from being favourable to his breed covering the ground exclusively, that they are actually much against his having any descendants at all alive, for though he has a rather better

chance of this than any of his neighbours, yet the chances are greatly against any one of them.[20]

For this objection, Darwin did not have a cogent answer. After all, he too accepted blending inheritance as the norm. As a result, Darwin had to justify his position by falling back on other arguments concerning sources of variation . . . arguments that rested much more on the inheritance of acquired characteristics that produced large and selectable changes in great numbers of individuals within a population. These were essentially arguments that could be seen as in agreement with the ideas of Jean-Baptiste Lamarck regarding the nature and inheritance of acquired traits. Although Darwin did not agree with Lamarck in general, he was, in some sense, forced to defend his theory in this way. What a difference it would have made if he had only known what was taking place at that same time in the garden of the monastery of St. Thomas in Brün, Austria.

GREGOR MENDEL AND GENETICS

The monastery of St. Thomas in the Moravian city of Brün was not at all what most people would picture. It was not a cloistered place of silent monks, going about their daily menial tasks in quiet prayer. Instead it was closer to what we might call a research institute. Most of the Augustinian friars who were there were scholars in some field, and each held a teaching post at one or another local schools. Some were mathematicians, physicists, philosophers, and musicians. At least two were botanists: the abbot, Fr. Napp, and the young friar, Gregor Johann Mendel.

The achievement of Gregor Mendel cannot be underestimated. In many ways, like Darwin, he saw beyond the limitations of the science of his time. In another way, unlike Darwin, he did not have the receptive audience of, say, the London intellectual community to promote his work. In addition, unlike Darwin, the scientific community was not ready to accept the paradigm shift that his results represented.

Mendel discovered and documented that inheritance, rather than being a blending of parental traits, actually involved the passing on of discrete, particulate determinants of the traits, what we now call genes. Rather than being the "paint pot" model of blending, Mendelian inheritance involved the preservation of these particulate features, even when they are not apparent in the appearance of the offspring. As a result, the variations that Darwin was trying to argue would be the targets of natural selection would not be swamped out but rather present in subsequent generations and ultimately available to be fully expressed under the right circumstances.

Mendel, as every historian of science knows, carried out his initial work with the common garden or sweet pea. These results were first presented in 1865 before the Brün Society for Natural Sciences and later published in their proceedings. The power of the experiments was that, for the first time, someone applied quantitative analysis to the outcome of manipulated plant crosses. As a result, Mendel was able to discern the rules by which inheritance takes place. These regular behaviors, now called "laws of genetics" because of their invariability, lead him to the conclusion that traits are associated with what he knew to be units of inheritance. The data were convincing and the results were clear. Why did this not have the same impact as the publication of *Origin* a few years earlier?

First, the scientific, specifically biological, community was not prepared to accept these results. No one understood the cellular mechanisms that were involved in reproduction. In fact, the basic structures in cells responsible for inheritance, the chromosomes, were not observed until 1042, and their function during cell division was not clearly understood until the very end of the nineteenth century. As a result, the idea that anything in the cell behaved in the same fashion as Mendel's particles of inheritance was out of the question at the time his work was published.

Second, Mendel actually had difficulty repeating his pea experiments with other plant species. He worked with the hawkweed plant and could not produce the kind of stable results he had found with the sweet pea. It was because of this that the eminent botanist, Carl Nägeli at the University of Munich could not agree with the theory Mendel set forth. The result was that though Darwin might read of Mendel as an experimenter in plant hybridization (Mendel is mentioned briefly in this regard in two books that Darwin acquired late in his life), there was no way that Darwin could have been aware of the ultimate importance of his results.

Mendel's achievement was recovered at the beginning of the twentieth century, when Hugo DeVries, Franz Correns, Erich Tschermak, and William Bateson all pointed toward his work and his 1866 paper as the foundational material of the new field of genetics.

DARWIN, MENDEL,
AND THE TWENTIETH CENTURY

Curiously, the decade from 1859 to 1869 saw three scientific events that, at the time, seemed to have absolutely no bearing on each other. The year 1859, of course, marked the publication of *Origin*; 1866, as we have seen above, was the date of publication for Mendel's conclusions from his pea hybridization experiments. And in 1869, Friedrich Miescher, working in Tübingen, isolated a substance he called nuclein from white blood cells. This has come to be called DNA.

No one at the time had any inkling that these three scientific events had any relationship to one another. However, by the middle of the twentieth century, Darwinian evolution, Mendelian genetics, and concepts about the structure of genetic information (DNA) and its mutation would be brought together to make what Julian Huxley called "the new synthesis" or the neo-Darwinian paradigm.

Darwin's dilemma that could not resolve how traits could survive the passage of generations and how natural selection could act upon them was solved. Traits are not blended but rather inherited in a particulate fashion as regions of DNA. And DNA itself can undergo changes called mutations, leading to variations in these traits. It is this process, over geological time, that the neo-Darwinian synthesis views as the source of Darwin's gradual variations. Natural selection, his proposed force that drives the evolutionary process of speciation, acts upon this pool of variants by allowing reproduction and subsequent passage of those advantageous mutations on to future generations, allowing a population of organisms to change over time . . . that is, to evolve.

THE "ECLIPSE OF DARWIN"

Even though scientists around the world voraciously read *Origin* in the final decades of the nineteenth century and the opening of the twentieth, they did not uniformly endorse natural selection as the mechanism for evolution. The principle of natural selection was random, accidental, contingent. It describes nature engaging in trial-and-error. Strict reliance on natural selection expunges the idea that design or purpose or direction or progress can be discerned within biology.

The nineteenth century was an optimistic century. Nearly everyone believed in progress. People had seen progress in industrial expansion, scientific discovery, and technological advance. Change over time had come to mean progress, betterment, and improvement. Could social progress apply to nature? Or, to reverse the logic: could our social progress be rooted in a previous progress built into nature? Might we understand biological evolution as progressive? How could it be otherwise?

As persuasive as Darwin's arguments in *Origin* were, they fell short of utterly convincing the wider scientific community. Even Darwin's closest colleagues, Thomas Huxley and Herbert Spencer, could endorse Darwin's theory in general but were hesitant to accept the lack of progress implied by the law of natural selection. A variety of alternatives to Darwin grew up within the comprehensive garden of evolutionary thought.

It was Julian Huxley, grandson of Thomas Huxley, who coined the term, the "eclipse of Darwinism," to designate that period after the publication of *Origin* when a number of alternative versions of evolution—many incorporating the doctrine of progress—were vying for the scientist's approval. When the field of genetics was added to the mix, providing a strictly natural explanation for variation in inheritance, then the eclipse was over. The neo-Darwinian synthesis became selected, and the idea of progress in evolution went extinct. Historian of science Peter J. Bowler comments: "In the end, genetics would destroy the credibility of the main alternatives to Darwinism and provide a new foundation for the selection theory."[21] The neo-Darwinians—those who combine genetic inheritance with natural selection—actually retrieved the original Darwin, the Darwin who relied on natural selection as random and nondirected.

WHY DOES DARWIN'S MODEL REPRESENT THE BEST SCIENCE EVEN TODAY?

The neo-Darwinian paradigm has become the overarching principle for all of biology, from the biochemical to the population level. It fits the definition of the best science in three ways. First, it is a model that has great explanatory power. Observations ranging from the fossil record to phylogenetics to DNA and protein sequence data all support the notion of common descent with modification.

Second, Darwin's evolutionary model is extraordinarily fertile or fruitful. It meets the criterion of fertility because it suggests new pathways of discovery that are still being explored. The model is progressive; it suggests roads to be followed that will lead to new knowledge. The journal *Science*, in December 2005, named biological evolution as the "breakthrough of the year."[22] In the introduction to this announcement, the journalists stated:

> Today evolution is the foundation of all biology, so basic and all-pervasive that scientists sometimes take its importance for granted. At some level every discovery in biology and medicine rests on it, in much the same way that all terrestrial vertebrates can trace their ancestry back to the first bold fishes to explore land. Each year, researchers worldwide discover enough extraordinary findings tied to evolutionary thinking to fill a book many times as thick as all of Darwin's works put together.[23]

This is the kind of fruitfulness that marks a fertile scientific model. Everything from the identification of genetic changes that mark speciation events in stickleback fish, to the understanding of relatedness between the human and chimpanzee genomes, to building strategies to stave off potentially lethal forms of the influenza virus . . . all of these areas stem from and depend upon the neo-Darwinian model.

And yet, there is a third feature of good science that must be mentioned. A scientific theory or model must also be, in principle, open to revision or to replacement by a model with better explanatory power. That is to say that any good theory must be structured so one can assess whether new evidence supports or falsifies it. This means that when sufficient contrary data is accumulated, the model must respond either by being revised or by being supplanted by a new model.

And so, the Darwinian model must ultimately fulfill these requirements. True, Darwin's original proposal has been modified, supplemented, and argued about within the scientific community for the 150 years since it was first placed before us. To date, however, it remains the best explanatory device for the observed data and continues to generate new information and new lines of investigation. What might the future hold?

BIOLOGICAL EVOLUTION IN THE TWENTY-FIRST CENTURY AND BEYOND

Already, biological evolution is much different than Darwin might have imagined it, even though *Origin* contains some amazingly perceptive statements about the future.

The late Stephen Jay Gould was one of the most prolific contributors to the more recent changes that we have seen to the evolutionary model. Along with Niles Eldridge he proposed the concept of punctuated equilibrium.[24] While apparently in contradiction to Darwin's gradualism, it still has enriched the model by allowing us to account for seemingly incongruous features of the fossil record. By proposing that species go along in relative stasis for a period of time (in geologic terms) and then go through a relatively rapid period of divergence (again, in geologic terms), they were able to deal with observations made since Darwin's time as paleobiology expanded its reach into greater and greater details of the record.

And with Richard Lewontin, Gould attempted to critique strict adaptationism as the exclusive method by which evolution advances.[25] In proposing their "spandrel hypothesis" they were able to open our scientific vision in order to see a greater set of possibilities for how the incredible complexity of life might have evolved. This was not to say that the new proposal violated or contradicted the basic hypothesis of descent with modification . . . it merely challenged the notion of what natural processes might be taking place to effect it.

Critiques of evolution, especially those in the creationist or intelligent design (ID) camps, have attempted to make of Gould's work justification for their positions ("see . . . it's only a theory . . . they can't even agree among themselves"). However, nothing could be further from the truth. Gould was, indeed, a Darwinian. One need only page through his final book, his great masterpiece, *The Structure of Evolutionary Theory*, to appreciate the true understanding he had for Darwin's work.[26]

As this is written, other changes may be on the horizon. The most recent has been the understanding that genetic information does not necessarily flow in biological systems in the precise way that Mendel proposed—from parent to progeny. This vertical transfer is contrasted with horizontal gene transfer, such as occurs in the bacteria. It turns out that such transfer may be more widespread than originally assumed, even taking place with higher kinds of cells, perhaps mediated by the ubiquitous presence of viruses. The proposal has therefore been made that the very concept of species may have to be rethought.[27]

What will Darwin's theory look like in another 100 or 150 years? If we had to guess from the present trend, it will be modified but not abandoned. And yet, if history is any lesson, we could see Darwinian evolution become a special case, just as Newtonian or classical physics is a special case of the general nature of reality as modeled by quantum mechanics. Would this be possible? Would we really be talking about "classical evolution" as opposed to whatever the new and more all-encompassing model might be? The very nature of robust and productive science is such that the answer is yes, this is possible.

DRILLING THROUGH THE LAYERS OF IDEOLOGY

Thousands of feet below the surface of the earth lie rich deposits of petroleum, what some tycoons have called "black gold." This fluid, vital to the current world economy, has to be extracted with great effort. Wells are drilled through layers of rock until the oil bed is reached. Often, the oil is found permeating porous soil, such that the precious liquid needs to be squeezed out before it's brought to the surface for refining and use.

Like oil, the science of evolutionary biology lies buried beneath layers and layers of ideology. Like oil drilling, we need to penetrate beneath the layers of ideology in order to extract the black gold. The scientist needs to retrieve the biological principles of the nineteenth-century Charles Darwin, because these have continued to prove fertile for contemporary laboratory research. The theologian also needs to retrieve the actual science of evolution to avoid confusing what can genuinely be called science from the misleading ideologies that make it appear so threatening to religion. The following diagram (figure 2.1) indicates what we believe to be the state in which we find this science today.

The rich science of evolutionary biology, with all of its explanatory power and fruitfulness, needs to be extracted from under the layers of ideology with which it was covered almost immediately after the publication of *Origin*.

THE METHOD OF SCIENCE

One of the hallmarks of science, as it has developed in the modern era, is the method or approach used to understand the natural world. Very

FIGURE 2.1: *Evolution as It Relates to Ideology*

often, like children tinkering with a clock, we take things apart to see how they work. When we do this, we end up with a collection of pieces that we would like to think can be added back together to make the whole—the clock with which we started.

In philosophical terms, taking something apart into the pieces that make it up is called *reductionism*. In the normal course of science, especially the molecular disciplines in biology, this is simply the method used to open up the details of the object of study. For instance, when a molecular biologist extracts the DNA from a cell and then examines the sequence of nitrogenous bases that make up the linear sequence of information contained in that DNA, the method of reduction is being employed. This is a practical, almost empirical decision being made and does not have philosophical implications per se.

Suppose, however, that a scientist, looking at the results of his or her experiments, decides that this is actually the only kind of valid knowledge to be gained from living systems. Such a scientist might say, "I don't see anything else I need to know, except the sequence of the DNA." In this case, he or she is making a philosophical decision about the nature of knowledge to be gained from the experiments. To say that science provides the only kind of knowledge that exists is, in itself, not a scientific statement. It is a philosophical statement. To believe the statement is to believe an ideology. This ideology is called *epistemological reductionism*.

Suppose that, when these results are published, the scientist's peers react to this new knowledge by claiming that all there is about the living system is contained completely in the sequence of the DNA; there is nothing else but this material substance that constitutes what it means to be this living thing. In this case, the scientists are making a philosophical claim about the nature of the living thing. To say that all living things are physical or material and devoid of spirit or other dimensions constitutes an ideology. This goes beyond what can be said scientifically. This is called *ontological reductionism*. As a widespread ideology it is also called *materialism*.

In each case, the value of the science in question does not depend upon either of the two philosophical decisions. That is, the sequencing results for DNA are just that—a set of data about this molecule which can be explanatory and fruitful. The philosophical commitments have nothing to do with the empirical knowledge gained. In sum, good science employs *methodological reductionism*; but it betrays itself and becomes ideology if it becomes *epistemological reductionism* or even *ontological reductionism*.

This is what we mean about the science of evolution being imbedded in a matrix from which it needs to be carefully extracted. Just as the oil in our deposit permeates its porous substratum, so too the science of evolutionary biology is frequently found buried beneath, if not mixed together with, unnecessary layers of philosophical additions. It is difficult to appreciate the new knowledge gained through methodological reductionism when the unnecessary layers of epistemological or ontological reductionism hide what is genuinely scientific. However, we can see, once we have extracted the science, that it requires only the method, but not the philosophy.

Epistemological and ontological reductionism are the two ideologies that lie immediately on top of evolutionary biology. Yet, the black gold of this science is buried still deeper because of numerous other layers of ideology. Darwin's nineteenth-century theory, although derived by the method of science, immediately became the stimulus for philosophical, sociological, and theological interpretation. Drilling beneath these layers of interpretation is an arduous process that will require considerable effort. Here we go.

THE DOCTRINE OF PROGRESS

"Progress is our most important product," was once the advertising slogan of the General Electric Company. That progress exists in the human world is undeniable. Every day, engineers design new machines that hitherto never existed in the history of our planet. Technology builds upon previous technology, sometimes growing at breathtaking speed. The world is becoming a better place, we believe, because of the progress of science and its accompanying technology. And it just may seem that God is the author of this progress, at least according to the late nineteenth-century poet Pricilla Leonard in "The Will to Win."

> O mighty sea! thy message
> In changing spray is cast;
> Within God's plan of progress
> It matters not at last
> How wide the shores of evil,
> How strong the reefs of sin,
> The wave may be defeated
> But the tide is sure to win!

Yet, we ask: is there progress in nature? Does nature have a linear direction? Do new life forms develop according to a purpose, a design? Does the long history of biological evolution demonstrate an inherent principle of progress, an entelechy, a *telos*, a single-minded drive toward improvement if not perfection? If science and technology exhibit linear progress, might we find that biological evolution exhibits progress? Is progress something strictly human, or is human progress already an extension of what we have inherited from our biological past? Or, to put it another way, does the idea of progress constitute an ideological overlay—a doctrine—on top of evolutionary biology?

This is a much-debated topic. When the dust settles over the debate, it is our conclusion that progress is indeed an ideological overlay. The theory of evolution does not require the doctrine of progress applied to speciation; and many contemporary biologists deliberately eschew the doctrine of progress because it gets in the way, so to speak, of empirical research. The mind-set of methodological reductionism must bracket out progress when examining the evidence, even if believing in progress seems the sensible thing to do from a philosophical perspective.

The doctrine of progress was developed during the Enlightenment in

the century or two just prior to Charles Darwin. Western Europe had witnessed progress in the Industrial Revolution; so the concept of progress
was ready and handy. Might we apply progress to nature? To biological
evolution? The easy answer would be: yes. Nature progresses just as
human science and technology progress, so it seemed. The rise of science
took place in the Enlightenment era within which the doctrine of
progress guided human affairs.

What we are calling a doctrine of progress was already attached to the
scientific and philosophical worldviews just prior to the appearance of
Charles Darwin. The most influential position at the time was called *positivism*, developed by Auguste Comte. Progress and positivism came
together. Comte's book, published in 1856, set down the principles of this
philosophical approach. Its central tenet was that scientific knowledge is
the only valid kind of knowledge and that the scientific method proves
or "affirms" theories and therefore such theories can be seen as positive
statements about the way nature is. It was assumed that along with the
progress of scientific knowledge, comes progress for society overall.

Positivism celebrates the triumph of reason over what was then viewed
as superstition. Positivists held science in high regard. In fact, because
they viewed the scientific enterprise as a linear and continual increase in
our knowledge about the natural world, they also viewed societies as pro-
gressing toward greater and greater perfection. For the positivists, societies evolved from primitive superstition up through religion until they
reached their perfection in the age of reason, when they achieved scientific knowledge. The entire history of the human race, it appeared to the
nineteenth-century positivists, had been evolving in order to prepare the
way for scientific progress. Comte succinctly described how progress and
his positivist philosophy were linked in *A General View of Positivism*, published in 1848:

> In my *System of Positive Philosophy* both these objects were aimed at. I
> attempted, and in the opinion of the principal thinkers of our time suc-
> cessfully, to complete and at the same time co-ordinate Natural
> Philosophy, by establishing the general law of human development,
> social as well as intellectual. . . . Our speculations upon all subjects
> whatsoever, pass necessarily through three successive stages: a
> Theological stage, in which free play is given to spontaneous fictions
> admitting of no proof; the Metaphysical stage, characterised by the
> prevalence of personified abstractions or entities; lastly, the Positive
> stage, based upon an exact view of the real facts of the case. The first,

though purely provisional, is invariably the point from which we start; the third is the only permanent or normal state; the second has but a modifying or rather a solvent influence, which qualifies it for regulating the transition from the first stage to the third. We begin with theological Imagination, thence we pass through metaphysical Discussion, and we end at last with positive Demonstration. Thus by means of this one general law we are enabled to take a comprehensive and simultaneous view of the past, present, and future of Humanity.[1]

When Darwin appeared on the scene, one could ask: was such progress already taking place in biological evolution before the development of human rationality? Is modern science the result of a long evolutionary process that began with inanimate matter, continued through simple life forms to complex life forms, and finally attained life's intended stage of scientific reason? Does the doctrine of progress provide scientists with a way of congratulating themselves?

The theory of evolution was both a product of and an unwitting contributor to the positivist stance. To recapitulate, Darwin proposed that every living thing descended with modification from a common ancestor by means of natural selection. The positivist view would be that these modifications were all perfecting the function of the organism, and thus, passing through the crucible of selection was tantamount to being refined. The end result would be a creature that was better at what it did, whether that was seeing, running, swimming, or any other biological function. The tree of life was seen as one whose branches were not only higher in distance from the roots but also better or more perfected than from where they arose. At the ends of those branches the most beautiful flower would be intelligence, reason, the human mind. Life has progressed not only in time but also in functionality, becoming closer to the ideal.

When this same notion is applied to human societies, one can see that natural selection of social systems is only for the good, if what comes about is a more perfectly functioning organization. Science teaches this about nature, so why should it not become the guiding light for human organization? Should we construct a social ethic based on the progress we have allegedly observed in nature? Should we speed up the progress of evolution by orienting our cultural values, our social institutions, and even our government accordingly? Should we in the human race take future evolution into our own hands?

It is easy to see how, especially in the life sciences, the idea of progress is related to the obvious design and purpose in nature. Francisco Ayala, the evolutionary biologist and philosopher of science, has argued that Darwin's great contribution was not just the evolutionary model, but more important, the idea that design in nature was the result of natural phenomena governed by natural laws, and that this was something that could be subject to scientific investigation.[2]

Just what do we mean by "design" and "purpose" in this case? Ayala distinguished three kinds of situations that demand "purposeful" or "teleological" explanations: artificial (external) teleology, bounded natural (internal) teleology, and unbounded natural (internal) teleology. These are best understood by everyday examples. Suppose that Marty wants to go skiing today. He gets into his car and drives up the mountain to the resort. The action of driving, as well as the car itself, are examples of artificial teleology. That is, the action is the purposeful behavior of an agent, and the car is the end result of design by an agent.

Biologically, Marty can rely on both bounded and unbounded teleological explanations to make his ski trip a success. For instance, the explanation of how he has the thermostatic body regulation to keep himself warm, with the help of proper clothing, is an example of bounded teleology. The end state of a constant body temperature maintained due to homeostatic mechanisms is best explained this way.

Finally, Marty has the capability of putting on boots and skis, getting onto a chair lift, and executing appropriate moves on the surface of the snow. This is explained by the anatomical structures he possesses due to the evolutionary history of his species. This is an unbounded teleological explanation. Clearly, none of Marty's eukaryotic ancestors, nor even his primate ancestors, had the intention of skiing in the natural selection of leg or hand configurations. Skiing is just an outcome of these design elements that happen to have selective advantage over geological time.

The positivist approach was to see both the natural laws governing this process and at the same time to argue for progress in bringing Marty into being from his nonskiing ancestors. That is, they rejected the natural theologians who would argue that Marty was the result of a divine design but fully accepted the idea that nature progresses such that design becomes more beneficial.

So, just what is wrong with progress? How can we call this an ideological overlay, suggesting that it is problematical? It seems so automatic to think that the progress witnessed within the field of science could be projected onto the subject matter that scientists study, namely, biological evolution? Why would one want to drill beneath the layer of progress to get to the black gold of science?

First, positivism was excessively reductionistic. As a philosophical position, positivism not only celebrated the scientific method but also argued that the only valid form of knowledge was that gained by this method. Positivism embraced epistemological and even ontological reductionism. It was materialistic. It denied spirit, while affirming intelligence as a product of physical developments. In effect, positivism eliminated any religious worldview based on a metaphysical or theological commitment. The positivistic overlay made a judgment that went well beyond the limits of science, namely, that religious insight allegedly proffered false knowledge about nonexistent spiritual realities. In short, then, positivism was not itself science but rather an irreligious or even antireligious philosophical position.

Second, the application of apparent scientific progress to social systems commits the naturalistic fallacy. This fallacy is committed when one argues that what we find in nature dictates how we ought to behave. To base a moral "ought" on what "is" is to commit a logical fallacy. By definition, any "ought" takes us beyond what is in the present to a future we desire to be different and consider to be better. In the case of the nineteenth-century positivist doctrine of progress, the argument went like this: because biological nature progresses through evolution, we should copy nature and speed up the rate of progress in human society. However, for the human to emulate or copy nonhuman nature cannot help dehumanizing. Below we will describe briefly social Darwinism and eugenics, movements in which the naturalistic fallacy led to social disaster, even to genocide.

Third, the concept of progress becomes a substitute for religious trust in divine providence. Belief in providence had previously taken the form of trust that God would care for us. With progress, God would no longer be needed, because the promise of betterment is allegedly built right into nature. Faith in nature could replace faith in God. The marriage of progress with evolution constituted an annulment of the previous alliance of human faith with divine promise. "In the climate of the Victorian era the idea of *evolutionary progress* became a secular substitute for providence," writes Ian G. Barbour. "Blind fate was transformed into beneficent cosmic process, which was taken to guarantee the final fruition of history and even the perfectibility of man. Faith in progress replaced the doctrine of creation and providence as assurance that the universe is not really purposeless."[3] Although the doctrine of progress appears to be scientific, it is actually a disguised form of the religion it rejects.

Contrary to this cultural appropriation of evolution as progress, scientists who combined Darwin's model of evolution with the new genetics found they needed to distance themselves from progress. The genetic mutations that account for variations in inheritance are random. Natural selection is random. Nature advances by trial and error, not by design or direction. Contemporary scientists have come to believe that no progress can be seen in biology. Further, projecting progress or any degree of purpose into nature contaminates empirical research. Still, at the level of culture, the ideology of progress and the theory of evolution seem indistinguishable.

In the end a doctrine of progress is an ideological overlay, since with or without it the theory of evolution remains as a solid explanatory model with great fruitful value.

"I FINISHED YOUR BOOK YESTERDAY": ATHEISTIC MATERIALISM

Darwin's book was released for sale to the book trade on November 22, 1859. On November 23, Thomas Huxley wrote a letter to Darwin which began: "My dear Darwin: I finished your book yesterday a lucky examination having furnished me with a few hours of continuous leisure."[4] It is possible that Huxley had an advance copy, many of which were in circulation to selected scholars earlier that month. Nevertheless, the first edition comprised nearly five hundred pages. Finishing was quite impressive, even for an avid scholar such as Huxley.

Thomas H. Huxley was one of the most eminent intellectuals of Britain and, indeed, of nineteenth-century science. Huxley was interested in a wide variety of topics and, in spite of his lack of family resources, educated himself in science, history, and philosophy. He became a physician and ultimately an assistant surgeon on a royal naval ship, *H.M.S. Rattlesnake*. In 1846, like Darwin before him, Huxley sailed for what was to be a four-year voyage. Huxley, too, conducted scientific observations during this trip, succeeding well enough so that on his return he was accepted in London among the ranks of naturalists.

Darwin and Huxley became acquainted before the publication of *Origin*. Their written correspondence begins in July 1851 and continues until about three weeks before Darwin died on April 19, 1882.[5] The letters, which begin as professional exchanges ("My Dear Sir . . ."), ultimately become conversations between cherished colleagues and close friends.

Huxley was engaged in a career-long battle with the hegemony of the Anglican Church, especially when it came to a critique of the scientific worldview. His initial reading of Darwin's theory, along with his subsequent reflections, convinced him that this explanatory model for the development of the living world provided just the ammunition needed to strike a decisive blow against the ecclesiastical grip that ruled British society.

Huxley has been characterized by many sobriquets, not the least of which is "Darwin's bulldog," for his defense of the model. Most remembered is Huxley's bulldog bark during a debate with Bishop Samuel Wilberforce at Oxford in 1860. The snappy bishop asked Huxley whether he preferred to think of himself as descended from an ape on his grandmother's side or his grandfather's side. (One woman fainted, it is reported.) Huxley rose to the rhetorical occasion. He retorted that he would rather have an ape for an ancestor than a bishop.[6] Regardless of the disputed accuracy of this account, what emerged from this notorious debate was the humiliation of religious belief at the sound of scientific growling.

In the decades following the publication of *Origin*, it became clear that Huxley saw this as the beginning of a sea change in his struggle against the church. In fact, by 1880, in a talk given before the Royal Society, the text of which was printed in the newly founded American journal *Science*, Huxley used his religious terminology to describe what had become of Darwin's theory by that time.[7] He called evolution a "doctrine" and those working in the field "disciples" who were occupied in spreading and developing its "doctrines." This sentiment is echoed two generations later by Huxley's grandson, the evolutionary biologist Julian Huxley, who saw in evolution "the lineaments of a new religion."

Thomas Huxley invented the word *agnostic* to describe his position with respect to belief. Why not use the word "atheist"? For Huxley, the scholar, this was too conclusive. Perhaps it seemed too presumptive for a scientist. Rather say "I don't know" than espouse a defined position. However, materialists to this day understand his position and how he got to it from Darwin's work. Richard Dawkins says, in his book *The Blind Watchmaker*, "although atheism might have been *logically* tenable before Darwin, Darwin made it possible to be an intellectually fulfilled atheist."[8]

Despite his agnosticism bordering on atheism, Huxley's ethics did not turn callous or brutal. He did not recommend that human evolution follow the path already taken by biological evolution, according to which might makes right and only the fit survive. Rather, he embraced modern liberal values such as cooperation and peace. Huxley avoided the naturalistic fallacy, the fallacy of basing a moral "ought" on a natural "is."

"Darwin's Bulldog" was also known as "Evolution's High Priest."[9] In this role Huxley repudiated the notion that we could derive social ethics from nature's precedents. Even if survival of the fittest has been the law of evolution up until this point, it would debase the human spirit to make this our moral guide. The state of nature ought not become the state of civilization. We human beings have transcended the brutality of our evolutionary past, and we dare not appeal to survival of the fittest to justify temporary returns to that brutality. Even if the struggle to survive is a cosmic law, we must be of stout heart and establish a social order that defies that law.

Huxley rises to eloquence with his admonition to supplant survival of the fittest with "fitting as many as possible to survive."

> The practice of that which is ethically best—what we call goodness or virtue—involves a course of conduct which, in all respects, is opposed to that which leads to success in the cosmic struggle for existence. In place of ruthless self-assertion, it demands self-restraint; in place of thrusting aside, or treading down, all competitors, it requires that the individual shall not merely respect, but shall help his fellows; its influence is directed, not so much to the survival of the fittest, as to the fitting of as many as possible to survive.[10]

This atheistic ethic looks quite akin to a religious ethic.

Thus, immediately with the publication of *Origin* there occurred an overlay of antagonism toward religion, even atheism. This has developed into what is perhaps best termed *atheistic materialism.* The term "materialism" means that the only reality that exists is material, physical. There is no second level of reality, no spiritual dimension. If all of reality is strictly material, then no god plays a role in the course of natural events. Does the science given us by Darwin require atheistic materialism? No, it does not.

We notice that there is nothing inherent in the science of evolution that requires materialism or atheism as a presupposition. Darwin was simply proposing a naturalistic explanation for observations he and others had made. The agnosticism expressed initially by Huxley and the atheism currently articulated by Dawkins is a reaction to this explanation, not a requirement of it.

43

LET THE POOR DIE BY THE WAYSIDE: SOCIAL DARWINISM

Even though the ethics of Thomas Huxley sought to inspire human civilization to rise above its biologically inherited proclivities to violence, others turned to survival of the fittest as a model for human morality. Those who developed a social theory on the Darwinian model we remember now as the social Darwinists.

How do we know the difference between good and bad? Should we ask: how highly evolved is the behavior? To this question the social Darwinist would answer in the affirmative. "The conduct to which we apply the name good is the relatively more evolved conduct; and . . . bad is the name we apply to conduct which is relatively less evolved."[11] This is the core principle of evolutionary ethics as developed by Herbert Spencer. It is the foundation upon which social Darwinism was built.

The architect of social Darwinism was another giant of Victorian Britain, Herbert Spencer. Spencer's influence in philosophy, science, statistics, sociology, and psychology was unparalleled during the latter part of the nineteenth century. Born to a father who was already on a pathway to rejecting the influence of organized religion in his own life, Spencer was raised as a rather independent thinker. In his early life he bounced around from one occupation to another, spending time as a civil engineer, a journalist, and a magazine editor. He was eventually introduced into the elite intellectual circles of London and it was there that he met Thomas Huxley, John Stuart Mill, and, ultimately, Charles Darwin. He was greatly influenced by the positivist philosophy of August Comte and came to be a strong advocate of scientific progress. From his father, Spencer heard of the laissez-faire or free-market economics of Adam Smith. From his association with John Stuart Mill he came to understand the philosophical position of utilitarianism. And from the work of Auguste Comte he derived a conviction that the scientific method was the only valid way of gaining knowledge and that this enterprise of science would always be progressive.

Spencer, in an essay entitled "Progress: Its Laws and Cause," wrote about biological evolution at least two years prior to Darwin. However, Spencer's concept of how species evolve was dependent upon the ideas of Lamarck regarding transmission of acquired characteristics. After reading Darwin's work, however, he came to understand that natural selection was at work in the process. In fact, he coined his own phrase to describe this: survival of the fittest. Recall that Darwin incorporated this into the fifth edition of his work:

> I have called this principle, by which each slight variation, if useful, is preserved, by the term natural selection, in order to mark its relation to man's power of selection. But the expression often used by Mr. Herbert Spencer, of the Survival of the Fittest, is more accurate, and is sometimes equally convenient.[12]

In the story of the ideologies that overlay the science of evolution, Herbert Spencer is remembered most for his application of the Darwinian model to social systems. Although the late nineteenth century witnessed many theoreticians called "social Darwinists," Spencer's name is most closely associated with this extremely influential movement. The central tenet of social Darwinism is that human society obeys the laws of nature, the same laws Darwin identified in the history of biological evolution: the struggle for existence, selection, and survival of the fittest. The central ethical question became: should society voluntarily sharpen the struggle for existence to ensure more rapid progress, or should society seek to overcome our natural proclivity for competition with compassion and care for the weak and the suffering among us? Spencer and his disciples chose the first of these two, even while other social Darwinists elected the second.

Placing these influences alongside his own and Darwin's concepts of evolution led Spencer to suggest that, just as biological populations are subjected to selective pressures from which only the fittest will survive, so too social systems, both governmental and economic, would be subject to the same kind of evolutionary edict. The fittest would reproduce and have offspring, and the unfit would die off. Nature teaches us how society ought to behave. If we let the poor die by the wayside, the entire human race will progressively advance. If we intervene with programs of social welfare to help the poor, we will block nature's own refining process and retard evolutionary advance. What nature already tells us is what we should do.

Spencer opposed government programs to aid the poor. He also opposed state-supported education, regulation of housing conditions, tariffs, and even government postal services. Medical aid to sick young people before the age of reproduction, he worried, would risk perpetuating unfitness into the next generation and retard the larger progress of evolution.[13]

The poor are poor because they are unfit, Spencer told us. "The whole effort of nature is to get rid of such, to clear the world of them, and make room for better . . . it is best they should die."[14] Letting the unfit die along the roadside is the price we pay to ensure our larger society's progress: the unfit should be sacrificed so that the entire human race may progress in its evolutionary advance.

Although Spencer seems individualistic and even callous here, his ethical vision is more complex and nuanced than it might at first appear to be. Spencer is not simply importing to human society the brutality of animals or baptizing insensitivity to suffering. Rather, he is subordinating everything to a single pursuit of the good, a good that awaits us as we evolve further. When the human race arrives at its next stage in evolution, the social fabric will be more complex and include a higher level of altruism.

Spencer bases his future vision on the assumption that cosmic evolution over time leads to increased complexity, to a combination of increased heterogeneity and increased harmony. As life evolves, it becomes more diverse. When this diversity becomes reintegrated, the new level of integration will constitute a higher harmony. Some in this school of thought used the term *holism* to describe this integrative process.[15] Spencer defined "evolution" as the "integration of matter and motion," the process of breaking simple homogeneity with heterogeneity, followed by a new more highly developed homogeneity.[16] This is what happens in nature. What happens in human society follows this pattern. The heterogeneity among competing individuals that we see today will eventually be replaced by a higher degree of cooperation, by more altruistic behavior.[17] Egoism will give rise to altruism. To arrive at this more advanced stage, government should step out of the way, let the poor die by the way side (before they can reproduce more children of their own kind), and permit the natural processes of evolution to integrate the more fit who will have survived.

The titans of American capitalism found in Spencer a moral hero because social Darwinism could provide scientific justification for policies that would support the rich as they became even richer. If we leave the rich and the poor to compete with one another, the fittest will survive. More than survive, the fittest will become rich. Yale professor William Graham Sumner declared that the millionaire is a product of natural selection. To the previous authority of God could be added the authority of the laws of nature, laws that if obeyed guaranteed progress toward wealth. "The growth of a large business is merely a survival of the fittest," John D. Rockefeller told his Sunday school class. "It is merely the working out of a law of nature and a law of God."[18] As contrast and complement, Andrew Carnegie combined his rejection of belief in God with a naturalistic ethic to support the growth of big business. "Not only had I got rid of theology and the supernatural, but I had found the truth of evolution. 'All is well since all grows better,' became my motto."[19]

Not only did laissez-faire capitalism get a boost from evolutionary science, so did American imperialism. In 1898, John Barrett, U.S. ambassador to Siam, encouraged American rule over the countries in the Pacific Seas such as the Philippines by appealing to the image of survival of the fittest. "The rule of the survival of the fittest applies to nations as well as to the animal kingdom. It is a cruel, relentless principle being exercised in a cruel, relentless competition of mighty forces; and these will trample over us without sympathy or remorse unless we are trained to endure and strong enough to stand the pace."[20] President Theodore Roosevelt conveyed the same spirit in his 1899 exhortation, "The Strenuous Life." To conquer, Americans would have to be fit. "I preach to you, then, my countrymen, that our country calls not for the life of ease but for the life of strenuous endeavor. . . . If we stand idly by . . . then the bolder and stronger peoples will pass us by, and will win for themselves the domination of the world."[21]

Not only did laissez-faire capitalism and American imperialism get a boost from evolutionary science, so also did racial prejudice. The preexisting prejudice on the part of white Enlightenment Europeans—Anglo-Saxon and Teutonic peoples—against races of other continents perceived to be less civilized seemed to find scientific justification in social Darwinism.[22] Just prior to the publication of Darwin's *Origin*, the European and North American world was reading *Essai sur l'Inégalité des Races Humaines* (*Essay on the Inequality of the Human Race*), by Joseph Arthur Comte de Gobineau, which contended that racial competition is the driving force of world history. Competition between races was part of the cultural atmosphere within which Darwin worked, and it seeps into assumptions and assertions of his evolutionary theory. The lower races are "savages," and the higher races are "civilized." The lower races are less evolved, and the higher more evolved. And progress is guaranteed by the law of nature. In *The Descent of Man*, Darwin himself could write, "at some future period . . . the civilised races of man will almost certainly exterminate and replace throughout the world the savage races."

One French social Darwinist, Vacher de Lapouge, announced he would like to replace the slogan of the French Revolution—"liberty, equality, and fraternity"—with "determinism, inequality, and selection." One American social Darwinist, William Graham Sumner, said "nothing but might has ever made right." In Germany the hierarchization of the races according to an evolutionary calculus became even more intense. Ernst Haeckel, among others, contended that the competitive conflict between the races would only end with the extermination of the least fit races.[23]

Another key figure was Alfred Ploetz, who in the 1890s coined the term *Rassenhygiene* (racial hygiene). The human race as a whole, he argued, could be purified by evolutionary principles if we would simply deny medical attention to children under the age of puberty. We should allow only the healthy to live to the age of reproduction. If only the strong would give birth, the entire human race would advance in fitness. By the 1920s the concept of "racial hygiene" was used to distinguish the "more highly evolved" Nordic or Aryan race from the "less evolved" Jewish race, and German anti-Semitism found an apparent scientific justification in social Darwinism. This became the philosophical inheritance exploited by Adolph Hitler as he institutionalized *Rassenhygiene* during the Third Reich.[24] Social Darwinism provided the scientific justification for what we now call the "Holocaust," the systematic attempt by a government to exterminate the physically handicapped, the mentally retarded, homosexuals, and the Jewish and gypsy members of the population.

The creationists are sharply critical of Darwinism, because they believe Darwinian science is inextricable from social Darwinism. The science of Darwinism supports social Darwinism, they assume. And social Darwinism, complain the creationists, teaches a form of morality that is incompatible with the Christian emphasis on compassion, racial equality, economic justice, as well as charity toward the needy and the poor among us.

> The laissez-faire capitalism of the American industrialists was only one of the deadly fruits of evolutionary theory. . . . This was associated also with racism, the growing belief that the white race (some even narrowed this to the Teutonic race) had demonstrated its superiority in the struggle for existence and was thus destined to control or eliminate the other races. Neither imperialism nor racism originated with Darwinism, of course. . . . However, Darwinism finally provided racist imperialism with an apparent scientific justification.[25]

Although creationists are known for their biblical and scientific objections to Darwinian science, they no less strenuously argue against the values perpetrated on society by social Darwinism.

As this all too-brief review of social Darwinism shows, a thick layer of ideology covers the science of evolutionary biology. Already in Darwin's own era, chauvinistic theorists were pressing natural principles into service to justify self-serving social policies. In retrospect, social Darwinism appears immoral when viewed in light of contemporary commitments to racial equality and economic justice. Yet, the underlying science in *Origin of Species* that has led to the neo-Darwinian synthesis is indispensible for today's laboratory researchers. So we ask: can we have Darwin without social Darwinism? Can we benefit from Darwin's science even if we affirm human equality and social justice? Yes. Historian Richard Hofstadter contends that "Darwinism . . . was a neutral instrument, capable of supporting opposite ideologies."[26] To get to the black gold of Darwinian biology, we need to drill beneath social Darwinism.

DARWIN'S COUSIN: EUGENICS

Of course, many of the leading scholars reacted positively to Darwin's publication. Here's a sample of one such personal reaction:

> The publication in 1859 of the *Origin of Species* by Charles Darwin made a marked epoch in my own mental development, as it did in that of human thought generally. Its effect was to demolish a multitude of dogmatic barriers by a single stroke, and to arouse a spirit of rebellion against all ancient authorities whose positive and unauthenticated statements were contradicted by modern science.[27]

Like many intellectuals of the day, this writer saw in the theory more than just the science. Unlike many, however, this was one of Darwin's own family.

Francis Galton was perhaps more famous in his time than either Charles Darwin, his cousin, or Thomas Huxley. Galton was considered a polymath—an expert in a wide range of disciplines. He was an explorer, a companion of Sir Richard Burton trekking through Africa. He was a meteorologist, pioneering the use of weather maps. He was the first to propose the use of fingerprints as a forensic tool.

Most important, however, he read his cousin's book and then, in 1869, published his own widely read treatise, *Hereditary Genius*, in which he proposed that improvement of the human race could be accomplished by selective breeding. He gave the name *eugenics* to this new approach to controlling our own evolutionary future. He wrote:

I propose to show in this book that a man's natural abilities are derived by inheritance, under exactly the same limitations as are the form and physical features of the whole organic world. Consequently, as it is easy, notwithstanding those limitations, to obtain by careful selection a permanent breed of dogs or horses gifted with peculiar powers of running, or of doing anything else, so it would be quite practicable to produce a highly-gifted race of men by judicious marriages during several consecutive generations.[28]

What Galton proposed is that, if his cousin's theory is correct, then the traits of parents are passed on to offspring if those traits give a reproductive advantage to the parents. Therefore, he reasoned, we, being intelligent creatures, should be able to influence this process such that we improve our own species in a purposeful manner. This could be done in two ways. First, by encouraging the "best" among us to have more children. This is called positive eugenics. Second, by preventing the "worst" among us from having children. This is called negative eugenics.

Who are the "best" or the "fit" and who are the "worst" or the "unfit?" Galton attempts a definition of this in his book. Are we at all surprised to learn that the "best and the brightest" are, in fact, the British upper class? On his scale, everyone else rates lower, on down to Africans and other indigenous people. The unfit would also include people with mental defects, physically handicapped, and even those at the lower rungs of the socioeconomic ladder.

Eugenics was embraced by the scientific community, not only in Britain, but worldwide, especially in the United States. The Dolan DNA Learning Center at Cold Spring Harbor Laboratories in New York has produced a fascinating website containing a vast collection of information about the American eugenics movement.[29] This is an interesting quirk of scientific history, given that the original founding of the Cold Spring Harbor was as the principal eugenics center in the United States.

Proponents of eugenics in the United States practiced both positive and negative versions. In the first kind of eugenics, state fairs held "fitter families contests" and awarded prizes to the "best." On the other side, eugenics initiatives resulted in the oppression of those deemed to be "unfit," for reasons that were not at all scientifically based. The results were sterilization laws and marriage laws. Perhaps one of the most infamous cases was *Buck v. Bell*. Carrie Buck, a presumed "mental defective," was scheduled for sterilization by the state of Virginia. An appeal was mounted on her behalf and the case was eventually heard by the U.S.

Supreme Court. The Court ruled in favor of the state, with Justice Oliver Wendell Holmes Jr. writing the opinion. His words live today as a frightening example of the misapplication of genetics:

> It is better for all the world if, instead of waiting to execute degenerate offspring for crime or to let them starve for their imbecility, society can prevent those who are manifestly unfit from continuing their kind. . . . Three generations of imbeciles are enough.[30]

Eventually the practice of eugenics spread throughout western Europe, including Germany. It was here that the imprisoned Adolph Hitler, writing the book that would guide Germany into national socialism and into World War II, *Mein Kampf (My Struggle)*, incorporated social Darwinism and eugenics into his nationalistic ideology. Hitler appealed to the "iron logic of Nature," when arguing that "the stronger must dominate and not blend with the weaker . . . for if this law did not prevail, any conceivable higher development of organic living beings would be unthinkable."[31] Hitler adopted the concept of *Rassenhygiene* or "racial hygiene," and when the Nazis came to power he entrusted the S.S. to carry out an extermination program of all those persons who would hold back the evolutionary advance of the Nordic race. When Hitler combined the "struggle for life" with the "survival of the fittest," this resulted "in a sort of eschatological Darwinism," says Joachim C. Fest. Hitler "boasted of his intention of marching over Europe in great 'blood-based fishing expeditions' to help blond, pale-skinned human material 'spread its blood' and thereby win dominance."[32]

The end result of Hitler's dominance in Germany was the implementation of his own horrific takes on social Darwinism, eugenics, and genetics. Millions died in the name of protecting and improving the German race. In the face of the world's revulsion and the exposure of the extent to which the Nazis had gone, eugenics became a dirty word. Today, even the suggestion that some new medical technique that sounds like eugenics—such as the selection of the "best" embryos after *in vitro* fertilization (IVF)—will bring a chorus of outrage from the German populace. The memory of Nazi death camps is seared into the contemporary mind.

Yet, before we proceed to the next topic, let us ponder this for a moment. We need to point out that the contemporary selection of embryos in IVF clinics differs significantly from the eugenics programs of Galton or Hitler. The objective of today's genetic selection is the health or even enhancement of the baby to be born. The objective is not the evolutionary improvement of the human race as a whole. We can imagine, however, a scenario in which genetic services become a medical product sold on the open market. If large numbers of families engage in genetic selection for their children, trends might begin to take hold. Many newborns might find themselves with similar preferred genomes. Might the result be *freemarket* eugenics? Whereas the Nazis enforced eugenics by government mandate, might tomorrow's society find itself with a eugenics program sponsored by advertising and market demand?

Would freemarket eugenics worry our ethicists? Many among today's medical ethicists see the specter of "good breeding" in the theoretical possibilities of selecting children for good health, eye or hair color, intelligence, or for certain other physical attributes. The potential for this has been explored in fiction, from Aldous Huxley's two novels *Brave New World* and *Ape and Essence* to the recent Hollywood treatment by the director Andrew Niccol, GATTACA. Eugenics is not just a closed chapter in our history.

WHAT DOES DARWIN SAY ABOUT ALL OF THIS IN *ORIGIN OF SPECIES?*

Since we are in the mode of commenting on Darwin's *Origin of Species*, it is important for us to look to this text to see if any of these ideological positions are part and parcel of the scientific theory or model that is being presented. When Darwin revised his text for the sixth and final edition, he would have already understood the positions taken by Huxley, Spencer, and his cousin, Galton. If, as some modern commentators would hold, these ideological positions are intimately entwined with the evolutionary model, then we might expect that Darwin would have used them to support his case for acceptance of biological evolution.

Well, then, did Darwin refer to these three in the sixth edition? It turns out that he mentions Thomas Huxley five times, Herbert Spencer five times, and his cousin Francis Galton not at all. In one of Darwin's other works, *The Descent of Man*, Galton is referenced nine times. In fact, throughout this book Darwin refers to his cousin's book, *Hereditary Genius*, as a "great work." Most of the references in *Descent of Man* are to Galton's ideas about inheritance. Recall that this book was written in 1871, at a time when Mendel's understanding of heredity had not yet been accepted. And so, Darwin used these pre-Mendelian ideas found in

Galton's book and prevalent in much of the scientific mind-set of the day.

It is interesting to look at the ten references to Huxley and Spencer in the sixth edition of *Origin*. Here they are, in tabular form, by chapter, page number, and topic referenced:

	Chapter	Page #	Reference
Huxley			
	Historical Sketch	25	1859 lecture supporting descent with modification from an ancestral type.
	IV	105	Opinion about reproductive organs of hermaphroditic animals.
	XI	332	Comment on the placement of certain fossil remains as ancestral to whales.
	XIV	417	Comment on developmental origin of various organismic structures.
	XIV	421	Allusion to developmental drawings of bees to show various stages.
Spencer			
	Historical Sketch	23	1852 essay proposing his own theory of evolution.
	III	75	Use of phrase "survival of fittest" and attribution to Spencer.
	IV	127	Argument against Spencer's idea of evolution proceeding by Lamarckian mechanisms.
	IX	280	Comments on the idea of equilibrium in nature and forces involved in changing this situation.
	XV	458	Comment on evolutionary foundations of psychology.

Virtually all of these references are to the scientific achievements of Huxley or Spencer. None of them refer to their writings on agnosticism, on the one hand, or what we have come to call social Darwinism on the other hand. The 1859 Huxley lecture mentioned in the *Historical Sketch* section contrasts a creationist view with an evolutionary one, but it does not specifically rule out belief in God, or require disbelief as a prerequisite for accepting the science of biological evolution.

Certain modern commentators wish to argue that one of these ideological positions, atheistic materialism, is actually required by the neo-Darwinian paradigm. However, we find no evidence of this, either in the sixth edition of *Origin of Species*, which lays out Darwin's final thoughts about his model, or in any of the scientific developments that followed. Stated in another, more personal way, when Marty Hewlett goes into his laboratory to examine the molecular nature of viruses and their place in the biosphere, there is no necessity for him to abandon belief in God as a part of the scientific method he employs or in order to interpret the data he gathers. The evolutionary model works as an explanatory and predictive device, irrespective of whether the scientist in question is a theist or an atheist.

We have shown that atheistic materialism, social Darwinism, and eugenics are not mentioned as supportive positions in the sixth and last edition of *Origin of Species*. What about the doctrine of progress?

Origin was written at a time when positivism was becoming the accepted philosophical position for science and philosophers of science. Physics, after all, had answered all of the questions using the Newtonian perspective. Although Comte's book was published a mere three years before Darwin's, these ideas were pervasive in the Western academy. As a result, it is not at all surprising that Darwin would have taken a progressive view of his model.

Origin is full of arguments that relate to progress in the sense we have discussed. In each case, Darwin appears to reject a specifically positivist view, in favor of one that is more consistent with his theory. For instance, in chapter 7, "Miscellaneous Objections to the Theory of Natural Selection," Darwin confronts one of his most serious criticisms, from his German colleague, Heinrich Bronn. Bronn argued that features of organisms that did not seem to confer an obvious advantage, such as length of tails or ears, could not have been subject to natural selection. Instead, he argued for a progressive development, an idea promoted by the botanist Karl Nageli, where creatures had some innate tendency toward perfection. This view is obviously in the positivist, if not vitalist, mode. Interestingly, Darwin argues against this position by cautioning against the assumption that, just because the advantage of a structure is not apparent, this does not mean that such an advantage did not exist through the evolutionary history of the organism. Darwin holds that changes in the structure of organisms don't happen just for the sake of perfection. He says:

> There must be some efficient cause for each slight individual difference, as well as for more strongly marked variations which occasionally arise; and if the unknown cause were to act persistently, it is almost certain that all the individuals of the species would be similarly modified.[33]

In spite of Darwin's minimal defense of his theory against the idea of progressive development, it is still the case that the overall move of biological evolution was seen by him as in the direction of improvement, if not perfection. "Man in the distant future will be a far more perfect creature than he now is," Darwin wrote in his autobiography.[34] Even though he holds that the process is driven by natural selection rather than innate tendencies, there is still a largely positivist flavor to the work. Even in his famous "tangled bank" conclusion at the end of the book, Darwin refers to the "extinction of less-improved forms," implying that natural selection has pushed living systems in the direction of perfection.[35] Perhaps Darwin himself was less convinced than his contemporary disciples that the principle of randomness in inherited variation and natural selection precludes the doctrine of progress. Darwin's legacy is one of ambiguity regarding progress, an ambiguity later resolved by a commitment to evolution without progress made by many contemporary scientists.

However, the contemporary view of biology is that the result of biological evolution observed in the living world around us is just one of many possible outcomes. As Stephen Jay Gould wrote in his book, *Wonderful Life*,[36] if we reran the tape of evolution, it is unlikely that we would get the same thing. This concept of the structure of life being contingent upon the selective conditions present at any given time reflects Darwin's theory without the necessity of invoking progress toward the good, as we define it.

CHAPTER THREE

THE MANY THEOLOGIES OF EVOLUTION

Does Charles Darwin's theory of evolution mean that God is now out of a job? Does it mean that the structure of each species is solely the result of random variation and natural selection, and not the result of divine design? Does it mean the intricacy and beauty and majesty we witness in this magnificent world should no longer be thought of as the handiwork of a creator's artistry?

Questions regarding the theological significance of Darwin's sole reliance on naturalistic explanations were already raised during Darwin's own publishing career. Many of the issues encountered during the late nineteenth century are still with us today.

Three of these issues led to responses by Darwin in the sixth edition of *The Origin of Species*: the question of the special creation of each species; the question of design in nature; and the question of transitional forms. We will look at each multiple times in this introduction.

We need to point out first, however, that these three issues are but trees in a much larger forest. The larger forest is the overall question: how is God involved or not involved in the processes of nature? It appeared to many of Darwin's first readers that he had eliminated divine causation as a factor determining the world we observe through scientific lenses. Does this make science godless? Both Darwin's friends and opponents were inclined to answer: yes, Darwin's science is godless. God became absent from scientific explanations. Nature explains nature. No appeal to divine action would enhance a strictly naturalistic explanation for natural phenomena. The Darwinians, as Laplace before them, found they had no need for the God hypothesis.

The removal of the God hypothesis is upsetting to the religious mind for two reasons. First, when looking at the natural world through religious lenses, what we see is a beauty and elegance that befits a divine creator. Yet, as we have just mentioned, scientific explanations seem to eliminate God as a factor in nature's creative processes. The second reason is even more upsetting: the picture of nature drawn by the Darwinian model is grim and graceless. If speciation is driven by the ruthless law of survival of the fittest, then the natural world begins to look like the world that Alfred Lord Tennyson described in 1850: blood "red in tooth and claw." The violence inherent in the predator-prey interaction combined with the necessary death of myriads of sentient creatures and even the extinction of entire species does not befit a loving creator God.

Regarding the first upsetting matter, Darwin sought to comfort religious people regarding the existence of God, the world's creator. The theory of evolution does not necessitate denial of God's existence. It does not require a scientist to become an atheist. In the definitive sixth and final edition, Darwin writes:

> I see no good reasons why the views given in this volume should shock the religious feelings of any one. It is satisfactory, as showing how transient such impressions are, to remember that the greatest discovery ever made by man, namely, the law of the attraction of gravity, was also attacked by Leibnitz, "as subversive of natural, and inferentially of revealed, religion." A celebrated author and divine has written to me that "he has gradually learned to see that it is just as noble a conception of the Deity to believe that He created a few original forms capable of self-development into other and needful forms, as to believe that He required a fresh act of creation to supply the voids caused by the action of His laws."[1]

The approach Darwin takes here is to assign to God the job of bringing the creation into existence in the first place and even of originating life itself. These works could be ascribed to God as primary cause. Once we have life, then the course of evolution takes over and is governed by secondary causes, by natural causes. Principles such as random variation and natural selection belong to nature's realm of secondary causation. The "created forms of life . . . are produced by secondary laws," he writes.[2] By committing himself to what we earlier called *methodological reductionism*, Darwin can offer strictly natural explanations without eliminating God from the larger vision. Darwin's picture of the natural realm could be placed within a larger theological frame. In principle, one can believe in God as creator and still affirm evolution as an explanatory theory for speciation.

When we turn to the second matter—questions raised by suffering and death and evil in nature—we note how these also troubled Darwin. He recognized painfully the implications of nature's ruthless disregard for sentience. In a letter, Darwin wrote,

> I had no intention to write atheistically. But I own that I cannot see as plainly as others do, and as I should wish to do, evidence of design and beneficence on all sides of us. There seems to me too much misery in the world. I cannot persuade myself that a beneficent and omnipotent God would have designedly created the *Ichneumonidae* [insects whose larvae are usually internal parasites of other insect larvae] with the express intention of their feeding within the living bodies of caterpillars, or that a cat should play with mice.[3]

The violence of predation combined with massive extinctions led Darwin to use the term "waste" to describe nature's debris. Could waste on such a scale be reconciled with the idea that a loving God designed these natural processes? No. According to Darwin, it would be better to attribute it to natural processes than to divine design.

"The total amount of suffering per year in the natural world is beyond all decent contemplation," writes contemporary philosopher of science, Michael Ruse.

> During the minute it takes me to compose this sentence, thousands of animals are being eaten alive; others are running for their lives, whimpering with fear; others are being slowly devoured from within by rasping parasites; thousands of all kinds are dying of starvation, thirst, and disease. It must be so.[4]

Just how should we interpret this theologically? Is God responsible for all this violence, this suffering, this waste? Or, because "it must be so," should we think of nature as morally neutral? Should we simply stop our sentimental whimpering and let nature be what it is? Should we stop judging nature by our moral categories? Should we deny that suffering is evil? Darwin's disciple, Thomas Huxley, also wrestled with this question, answering it by eliminating God—by affirming agnosticism if not full atheism—while decrying evil and suffering in nature. "Evil stares us in the face on all sides; that if anything is real, pain and sorrow and wrong are realities."[5] What is significant here is that neither Darwin nor Huxley answer this painful question by ascribing moral neutrality to nature. Suffering, death, and waste are evil, plain and simple. What they add in their respective ways is the claim that God is not responsible for natural evil.

We now turn to three contemporary theological positions that respond to the challenges posed by Charles Darwin's theory of evolution. Because of these implications, the schools of creationism and intelligent design (ID) find they must reject as unsatisfactory the reduction of natural phenomena to inherited variation combined with natural selection. This naturalistic explanation that leaves God out of the picture is incomplete, perhaps even wrong. A third school of thought, theistic evolution, has made its peace with naturalistic explanations and still finds a way to affirm a divine authorship and divine plot to the story of creation. We will look at these three theological reactions to the Darwinian model of evolution in sequence.

CREATIONISM: BIBLICAL AND SCIENTIFIC

Christians today (along with some Muslims) who oppose Darwinism come in two species, creationists, and intelligent design advocates. Among the creationists two subspecies have evolved, the biblical creationists and the scientific creationists. Biblical creationists and scientific creationists are frequently seen with each other, to be sure; but their arguments against Darwinism take different forms. The first argues on the basis of the Bible's authority; the second provides scientific arguments for the inadequacy of the Darwinian model.

For a strong voice in favor of biblical creationism, "Answers in Genesis" or AIG, provides a loud example. Headed by Australian Ken Ham, AIG has just opened a creationist theme park in Kentucky near Cincinnati. Its website reminds us that all knowledge or wisdom begins with the fear of the Lord (Proverbs 1:7).[6]

In what follows, we will focus more on the scientific creationists, especially the young Earth creationists, known as YECs. The Institute for Creation Research, near San Diego, is the most influential representative of this position.[7]

Scientific argumentation characterizes the scientific creationists. They identify themselves as *scientific*, not biblical, creationists. They argue against Darwinism because they believe the Darwinian model is inferior to their own model, "creation science." They are aggressive because they are fighting for the soul of civilization, to prevent our culture's deterioration into atheistic materialism and social Darwinism that leads to a subhuman morality. Despite their complaint about Darwinian ideology, creationists attack the scientific theory of evolution by denying that the evolution of species has happened.

What distinguishes the YECs is their belief that *the earth is less than ten thousand years old.* YECs try to refute the idea of deep time and that different species evolved gradually over long periods of time. The consensus among establishment scientists is that the earth is 4.5 billion years old; and the appearance of life first occurred about 3.8 billion years ago. YECs, in contrast, date the origin of Earth at only ten thousand years ago.

All creationists, including YECs, believe God created the world from nothing. Theologians refer to this in Latin with the phrase, *creatio ex nihilo.* This belief is not unusual. Virtually all Christians affirm this. *Creatio ex nihilo* does not contradict the theory of evolution, because evolution is not about the origin of the world or even of life. Evolutionary theory tries to explain how one species developed out of another, what we have come to call *macroevolution.*

Creationists deny that any macroevolution occurred. As every biology sophomore knows, one can witness microevolution occurring in a culture dish. Even creationists can affirm that evolution occurs within a species. What is so important to creationists is that species remain fixed. When reading Genesis, they see that God created ten different kinds of things. This word, "kind," becomes the equivalent of "species." This is where the word "creation" plays such an important role: God creates each species individually and specially. On this list is the human race: God creates the human race individually and specially, meaning that we humans did not evolve from the animals. So, YECs go to great length to repudiate the idea of macroevolution, of change from one species to another.

Creationists oppose the idea of common descent with modification. They oppose the Darwinian model on the grounds that the ideas *of mutation and natural selection are insufficient to explain the development of all living kinds from a single point of origin.* What creationists substitute for this natural explanation is the assertion that God created each species (each kind) as we see it today. No evolution from one species to another has occurred. This is the single most salient scientific point where creationists are anti-Darwin.

When it comes to scientific arguments raised against the Darwinian model, chief on the list is the alleged absence of transitional forms, what we popularly call the "missing links." If one species gradually gave way to a subsequent species and then died out, one would expect its fossil remains to chronicle the transition. Yet, claim the YECs, no such fossil record of transitional species has been found. Establishment scientists dispute this, to be sure; reporting the discovery of numerous transitional forms such as fossils of reptiles with wings that demonstrate evolution from sea creatures to flying creatures.

One of the implications of the creationist position is the rejection of common descent applied to humans and primates. Creationists assert that *apes and humans have separate ancestry*. Creationists assert that the human race was especially created by God, as a distinct kind. They refute the standard Darwinian argument that humanity was the result of natural selection from among a variety of prehuman higher primates. In addition, the entire human race is descended from a single pair of parents, Adam and Eve, say YECs. Ironically, current anthropological models, based on the analysis of human mitochondrial and Y-chromosome DNA, also argue that we descended from a small number of ancestral males and females. This is not at all to say that science agrees with Genesis, even though popular science writers have picked up on this model, calling these ancestors our "mitochondrial Eve" and "Y-chromosome Adam."

The significance of racial differences is extremely important; because it has enormous moral implications. Ethically as well as historically, creationists are adamant in affirming that all races and all ethnicities are united. No one race is allegedly more highly evolved than another, say creationists. Civilized Europeans are not superior to the so-called "savages." There is only one human race. Creationists fear that social Darwinists could support racial discrimination if they say that separate races descended from separate species of monkeys (polygenesis). Even if social Darwinists on the eve of the twentieth century might have held such a prejudicial view, we must point out that evolutionary theorists in the twenty-first century do not appeal to common descent to justify racism. The creationist objection certainly applies to the first century of Darwinism, but not to the ideologies of today's most adamant supporters of evolution. On the issue of racial equality, Darwinian atheists and Christian creationists would agree on the equality of all human persons, regardless of race.

Even though the fossil record seems to support the Darwinian model by demonstrating speciation in rock strata, YECs demur. Most creationists teach that *earth's geology is explained by catastrophism, including a worldwide flood*. Based on Genesis 6–8, flood geology provides an alternative explanation for the fossil record, an alternative to *uniformitarianism* that holds that fossils were formed at a uniform rate over deep time. Creationist *catastrophism* ascribes to Noah's flood, dated three to five thousand years before Abraham, the multitude of fossils in sedimentary rock. If the Darwinian model were correct, argue the creationists, then we would see a geological ladder with simple fossils at the bottom and human fossils at the top; and such a stratification would support the idea of evolution over deep time. However, what we find are fossils of all life forms at all levels. Therefore, the fossil record supports catastrophism, say creationists. On this point, Darwin's defenders contend that odd geological formations are due to shifting, and this explains why rock layers do not provide a nice neat ladder of time with all the fossils in their proper strata.

We need to emphasize here that YECs offer what they deem to be *scientific* arguments against the Darwinian model. Whether appealing to lack of transitional forms or catastrophism, YECs make appeals to science and not to the authority of the Bible. Regardless of whether this counts as good science, scientific creationists see themselves as making distinctively scientific arguments against the Darwinian model.

What about the fertile science beneath the layers of ideology? All creationists complain that Darwinism corrupts the morals of our civilization. What do they mean? Do creationists reject progress? No, not necessarily. Nearly everyone in Western culture affirms belief in progress. We would believe in progress with or without evolutionary theory. Charles Darwin presupposed progress; and his evolutionary theory reinforced the idea of progress. Curiously, however, today's scientists agree that no such thing as progress can be seen in the biology, even if the idea of evolution is used to support progress ideologically.

What energizes and angers the creationists are social Darwinism, eugenics, and atheistic materialism. In their view these ideological overlays have become cultural poisons that could corrupt our youth in schools. In the early twentieth century, the anti-Darwinists complained that these ideologies would lead to militarism, racial discrimination, and economic injustice. In recent decades they blame drug use, homosexuality, and promiscuity on cultural acceptance of evolution. In our judgment, the latter moral judgments seem to have little relationship to the former. It would be hard to justify blaming the average high school science teacher for corrupting our youth on such matters.

The position taken by today's creationist has precedent among the opponents to evolutionary theory that Darwin confronted in his own day.

A close reading of the sixth edition of *Origin* will reveal that occasionally he finds he must defend his theory against the idea of the special creation of each individual species. For example, Darwin defends his view that varieties within a species eventually become selected for and then themselves become a species. He notes that descent with modification is inconsonant with the view that each of today's species is the result of an independent creation.

> On the view that species are only strongly marked and permanent varieties, and that each species first existed as a variety, we can see why it is that no line of demarcation can be drawn between species, commonly supposed to have been produced by special acts of creation, and varieties which are acknowledged to have been produced by secondary laws.[8]

Elsewhere Darwin seems to lose patience and trumpets that the doctrine of special species creation "makes the works of God a mere mockery and deception."[9]

Darwin also takes up the issue of transitional forms, or missing links. If Darwin is correct in positing that variation in individual inheritance leads to population varieties within a species, and this leads gradually over long periods of time to the establishment of an entirely new species, evidence of the transitional variations that went extinct to make way for the new species should be available. Yet, it appeared already in Darwin's own time that too little evidence of transitional varieties can be found. Does this repudiate the theory? No, says Darwin; and he sets out to explain why.

The analysis of the problem created by the dearth of evidence for transitional forms becomes the centerpiece of the important sixth chapter of *Origins*, "Difficulties of the Theory." Much is said. Key is that Darwin grants that transitional varieties must have existed and gone extinct, even though most likely they existed for shorter periods of time than the duration of a distinct species. With this in mind, one would expect fewer traces of transitional varieties than of the species themselves. What Darwin looks forward to is increased research by geologists. He predicts that in time geologists will find some, though by no means all, transitional forms.

> If my theory be true, numberless intermediate varieties, linking closely together all the species of the same group, must assuredly have existed;

but the very process of natural selection constantly tends . . . to exterminate the parent-forms and the intermediate links. Consequently evidence of their former existence could be found only amongst fossil remains . . . in an extremely imperfect and intermittent record.[10]

In time, says Darwin confidently, geology will vindicate the theory. Darwin turned out to be right about this. The predictive power of Darwin's theory of evolution is being confirmed today. New discoveries of transitional forms are catalogued almost daily. This includes, among other examples, fossils of reptiles developing wings, marking the evolution from reptile to bird. This had been anticipated by Darwin when discussing the "affinities of extinct species" in chapter 11 of *Origin*. When today's creationists insist that no transitional forms have been discovered, they must be judged to be mistaken.

Rather than wait to find transitional forms, some biologists are trying to reconstruct the most likely intermediate or transitional forms in the laboratory. They construct an array of possible mutational paths, both adaptive and nonadaptive. They look for mutational pathways that could yield a fitness improvement; they look systematically at all possible trajectories. Somewhat surprisingly, the list of possible pathways to increased fitness is smaller than expected. This observation leads to this conclusion: "That only a few paths are favoured also implies that evolution might be more reproducible than is commonly perceived, or even be predictable."[11]

Let us ask: why do creationists put so much effort into repudiating a scientific theory that is a century and a half old. Why the passion? Why the energy? What is at stake? It is the gospel, the very life-giving heart of the Christian faith that seems to be at stake for the creationist. What is the gospel? Henry Morris, the recently deceased patriarch of the Institute for Creation Research (ICR), directs our eyes to Jesus Christ. "The Gospel focuses especially on the person and work of the Lord Jesus Christ, the incarnate Creator (John 1:1-3, 14), who died in our place for the sin of the world (John 1:29)," he writes. "An understanding of faith in His bodily resurrection requires an acknowledgement that only He has conquered death, and, therefore, that He is Lord of all, able and sure to restore the whole creation someday to its primeval perfection." Now, one might ask: Why would this claim about Jesus Christ come into conflict with evolutionary science? Why not affirm both?

It appears that the conflict between evolutionary theory and the Christian faith falls into the doctrine of creation. It is in the doctrine of creation that we find testimony that God is the creator of all reality and the author of life. The gospel associated with Jesus Christ normally appears under the doctrine of redemption, not creation. So, what's the problem? We should notice the identification of the Creator with the Savior in what Henry Morris says. Notice also the identification of redemption with the creation prior to the Fall. "Thus, the Gospel is based on the good news that Christ Himself is the true Creator of all things and the good news that He, therefore, is King of Kings and Lord of Lords, sovereign of the universe, coming again someday to purge all evil and consummate all His purposes in creation."[12] Creation and redemption through Christ make the challenge of evolution a christological matter.

Both biblical and scientific creationists find that the impersonal and cold-blooded interpretation of nature that is implied by the Darwinian model contradicts what Christians know about the love and grace of God, expressed both in creation and redemption. The immense problem of suffering and evil receives attention in the creationist rejection of evolutionary history. The waste due to the actions of predators and in extinction is as revolting to creationists as it was to Darwin. Henry Morris, one of the founders of this movement, writes:

> Evolution is inconsistent with God's nature of love. The supposed fact of evolution is best evidenced by the fossils, which eloquently speak of a harsh world, filled with storm and upheaval, disease and famine, struggle for existence and violent death. The accepted mechanism for inducing evolution is overpopulation and a natural selection through extermination of the weak and unfit. A loving God would surely have been more considerate of His creatures than this.[13]

Curiously, both Darwin and Morris agree on this point: the God of the Bible simply could not employ a long process such as Darwin describes "with all its randomness, wastefulness, and cruelty."[14]

INTELLIGENT DESIGN

Just what is the connection between fundamentalism, creationism, and the next school of thought we would like to discuss, intelligent design? A very brief history of anti-Darwinism might help to connect and distinguish them. Christian fundamentalists entered the story in the 1920s by taking a stand against the teaching of evolution in public schools. Remnants of the "fight'n fundies" of the 1920s continue to spar today under the label of biblical creationism. The scientific creationists became a visible public force beginning in the late 1960s. ID advocates continued increasing their influence through the early 1980s, with residual influence into the mid-1990s. From the early 1990s to the present, ID has taken center stage. They have become the loudest anti-Darwinian voice; although that voice has been muted considerably since a legal setback in Dover, Pennsylvania, in 2006.

What does ID teach?[15] If we look at advanced biological forms, we see complexity, say ID advocates. Living beings are complex—that is, we cannot take them apart and reduce them to their chemicals and have them remain alive. This reduction would kill them. Complex living beings and biological systems within living beings are not like wooden walls. We cannot construct them with component elements like nailing boards on one another. More to the point, certain structures found in living systems, such as the human eye or the bacterial process, are so complex they could not possibly have come about by natural processes. They are irreducibly complex. So, how did they develop? How did they evolve? They could not have evolved gradually step-by-step through random genetic variation and natural selection. Complex systems in nature must be the result of a designer, an intelligent designer who is transcendent and who intervenes in natural evolution to scoot it along. This, in a nutshell, is the ID argument.

Intelligent design advocates ask us to look at the eye as an example. The component cells that make up the eye each have a different function. No cell individually sees. Only the complex system of cells provides sight for the organism. The eye is designed for sight. They argue that the eye could not have evolved gradually through uniform small increments of change resulting from random mutations and environmental selection. The entire complex system for seeing must have appeared at once. A designer who wanted creatures to see must have intervened to make this happen.

No one can read *Origin* without noticing how frequently Darwin alludes to such a design idea; and how he strives to repudiate it in favor of the law of gradual natural selection. The use of the eye as an example of complex design was an argument already pressed in the nineteenth century, and Darwin dealt with it explicitly. Darwin grants that the idea that the eye could have been formed gradually by small incremental changes seems at first absurd, to be sure; yet, a closer examination will vindicate natural selection as the best explanation. One can reconstruct the evolutionary history by observing that some nerves and epidermic cells are sensitive to light; and over time natural selection would incrementally add increased levels of complexity to improve the ability to see.

Key to sustaining Darwin's theory is the rejection of saltations: the rejection of sudden interventions by an intelligent designer. "If it could be demonstrated that any complex organ existed, which could not possibly have been formed by numerous, successive, slight modifications, my theory would absolutely break down. But I can find out no such case."[16] What ID theorists believe they have found here is the Achilles heel in Darwin's theory: saltations. So they press forward the need for saltations by a transcendent designer to account for leaps in complexity.

In light of today's science, however, IDs appeal to a transcendent designer to explain marvels of complexity such as the design of the eye avoids what the actual evidence offers. Biologists have gathered many primitive and partially developed forms of the eye from different species; and these demonstrate how the eye gradually evolved over time. One might also say theologically that ID trivializes God's work. If God intervenes in evolution to develop the eye, why do we still have to wear glasses? Is God less than a fully intelligent designer? What appears on the ID list of designs fails to include what is important to New Testament Christians, namely, God the redeemer heals. If God the redeemer had actually designed the eye, we would all have 20/20 vision.

Despite the attempt by ID advocates to advance a purportedly scientific explanation, this approach has a theological history. Thomas Aquinas, who lived in the twelfth century, noticed that some things we observe in the world behave as though they have a purpose. He argued that the idea of purpose for nature is an analogy for God's governance of the universe. He said that when you see things acting for a specific end, you might infer the governing action of God. Notice that he did not use the word "design." Nonetheless, later generations of scholars called his statement "the argument from design."

What we see among today's ID advocates is the substitution of design for governance, even though they refrain from applying the word "God." They refrain from identifying the intelligent designer; they limit their assertions to the presence of discernable purpose or design within complex natural phenomena. The result is that the ID position supports macroevolution understood as change over time. Still, ID denies that random variation and natural selection can provide an adequate explanation for the appearance of complexity in the natural world. Appeal to an intelligent designer provides a superior scientific explanation, ID contends.

Here is where the controversy gets hot. Defenders of Darwinism who take a strong stand against ID accuse it of being deceptively religious. Further, they accuse ID of being creationism in disguise. Opponents of ID embrace the following logic: If they can persuade the public that ID is creationism, then it would follow that ID is religious. If they can persuade the public that ID is religious, then it would follow that ID is not science. If religion in disguise, then ID can be excluded from public school science classes on the grounds that it violates the First Amendment to the U.S. Constitution that says the government cannot favor one religion over another. Some ID enemies use the term *intelligent design creationism* in an attempt to force the two into the same category. Intelligent design supporters vociferously deny that they are creationists, and they deny they are presenting a religious perspective. Rather, they claim to be providing a scientific model for the origin of species. When the controversy has entered the courtroom in cases dealing with public school science textbooks or curricular matters, the opponents of ID have most frequently won the day. The net result has been a widespread public impression that the Darwinian model supports an antireligious point of view if not outright atheism; and ID supporters seem to presume that the validity of the Christian faith is somehow dependent on destroying public confidence in the Darwinian theory of evolution. Even worse, the impression is left that the Christian faith is at war against science.

We would like to point out that, theologically, the ID position differs from that of the creationists. The creationists, as their name indicates, are concerned about creation—that is, they assert that God created all species in their respective "kinds" at the beginning. No macroevolution has taken place since the beginning of the world. Intelligent design is concerned about change within the already existing created order. Intelligent design finds it can accept something like macroevolution, but it adds that intelligent design rather than natural selection better explains macroevolution. Creationism denies that evolution takes place, whereas ID affirms evolution by offering an alternative to natural selection to explain evolution. This is quite a big difference. Both YECs and ID supporters claim to be making scientific arguments, even if on Sundays they find themselves sitting next to one another in evangelical churches.

Finally, despite its claims to provide an alternative science, in our judgment, ID does not qualify as explanatory science. By leaving holes for transcendence that naturalistic explanations are unable to identify, let alone plug up, ID's theory of nature makes law-like behavior unreliable. Science needs reliability in its explanation of law-governed natural phenomena.

In addition, ID does not provide us with a fertile research program. It does not stimulate the development of new knowledge. Intelligent design is not going to predict what will happen in nature; nor does it provide the kind of knowledge we need to develop new medicines based on those predictions. Neither creationism nor ID pass the test for what counts as the best science. The Christian faith demands the best science, and it is our assessment that neither creationism nor ID measure up to this standard.

JEWISH INTERESTS IN THE EVOLUTION CONTROVERSY

Now we might ask: Is the struggle to interpret the religious significance of Darwinian evolution strictly a Christian matter? Where might the Jewish community find itself on this matter?

To look at the controversy from a Jewish perspective, the battle over evolution looks like somebody else's war. It is not a Jewish problem. The Jewish understanding is that God's creation at the beginning was unfinished; so it is no surprise that a scientific theory such as evolution might arise that shows ongoing creation. In addition, the Hebrew concept of *Tikkun Olam*, according to which we in the human race are mandated by God to fix what is broken in creation, leads to the strong emphasis in Jewish culture on healing, including the scientific pursuit of medicine.

In the Jewish history of biblical interpretation, the tradition of *halakhah* permits and even encourages expansion from the literal character of God's revelation to the chosen people toward universal wisdom and shared knowledge. It permits and even encourages healthy hospitality to science. When modern science offers new understandings of the natural world, Jewish interpreters quickly incorporate this into their interpretation of God's work in creation. A conflict with the Darwinian model of evolution is less likely to arise in Judaism than in other religions of the Book.

Nevertheless, some Orthodox Jews see a conflict between the Darwinian model and allegiance to the biblical account of creation in the book of Genesis. Some Orthodox Jews find themselves in sympathy with Christian creationists and borrow Christian arguments. On balance, however, the dominant view of contemporary Judaism is to treat Genesis symbolically or figuratively, not literally; hence, relatively little difficulty with Darwinian evolution has arisen within Judaism.

MUSLIM INTERESTS IN THE EVOLUTION CONTROVERSY

Like Christianity, the religion of Islam was born in an ancient culture. We all have to mature in a world permeated with modern science. "God is the Creator of all things," says the Qur'an (13:16). Now, did God create once and for all, only at the beginning? Elsewhere we read: "Were we incapable of the first creation?" (50:15). Could this indicate a second creation or, better, continuous creation? Some Muslims, especially those educated in the West, think so. Westernized Muslims want to interpret the Qur'an in such a way that the road can be paved for evolutionary theory to travel right into the heart of Islamic theology.

Some Muslims welcome the incorporation of modern science, including evolution. Others oppose the idea that Islam can easily open its doors to evolutionary science. Why the opposition? Because such a science seems to be connected to materialist ideology. The atheistic materialism that so frequently accompanies evolutionary science denies the independent existence of the human mind, of spiritual reality, and even of God. The Islamic religious vision retains the independent existence of mind and spirit, as well as God. It is a perversion to say that mind simply evolved from a material base; and it is even a bigger perversion to deny that the creator God has a design operative in natural processes.

Among Turkish Muslims, some go still further down the anti-Darwinian road. Like America, a culture war between religion and secularism remains hot within Turkish society. The public school system insists on teaching a Darwinian model of evolution as the only approach to biology. A number of Muslims feel this constitutes a secular intrusion into their religious beliefs. They borrow many of the arguments raised by scientific creationists and ID advocates to use in the Turkish culture war.[17]

In summary, among today's Muslims we can find a spectrum. On one end, we locate Muslims who fully accept Darwinian evolution, complete with precedents identified in the Qur'an. In the middle, we can find toleration for the science with rejection of the materialist ideology. At the other end, we find rejection of Darwinian evolution parallel to what we find in creationism and ID.

CHRISTIAN THEISTIC EVOLUTION

Should Christians take a stand against Darwinism? One would think so if we listen only to what YECs and ID advocates say. The problem is that both suggest that to be Christian is to be opposed to Darwinism. The so-called Christian view is seen as antithetical to the Darwinian view. This is misleading, we believe. Why? Because for more than a century and a half many Christians have made their peace with the concept of evolution in general, and even the Darwinian model in particular. Those who both affirm their Christian faith and accept descent with modification within a framework of macroevolution are members of a noninstitutionalized school of thought that we will call *theistic evolution*.

The first chapter in the story of theistic evolution begins before Darwin published *Origin*. Already in the 1840s some liberal Christian theologians were seeking to integrate the evolutionary vision into their scheme of creation and redemption. God creates over time, they said; and biological life has already evolved to the point of bringing the human race into existence. Quite explicit in these versions of theistic evolution was belief in progress. Biological progress leads to social progress, moral progress, and spiritual progress. Liberal Christians allied themselves with social Darwinism and even eugenics. Like many scientists in the final half of the nineteenth century, theologians affirmed the significance of Darwin's contribution to the theory of evolution but persisted also to affirm progress. They insisted on progress despite its ambiguous support within *Origin*. When in the twentieth century the neo-Darwinian synthesis compelled the scientific community to acknowledge the lack of empirical support for progress, the nonprogressive stance became the accepted scientific stance. Any theistic evolutionists who had bet on progress had bet on the wrong horse.

Drawing upon the prior work of historian James R. Moore, Peter J. Bowler observes how in the late nineteenth and early twentieth centuries:

there seems little difference between secular Darwinists and liberal theologians, who also accepted evolutionism. Both shared the assumption that evolution was progressive and purposeful, driving life up the scale of mental and physical development until eventually the human race appeared. . . . To make this assumption of progress work, however, the first generation of Darwinists had to evade the radical implications of the selection theory, which the conservatives—quite rightly—identified as difficult to reconcile with religion. . . . In this respect, then, the earlier debate was not a rehearsal for the modern conflicts. Darwinism was seldom promoted in its most radical form, and the apparently black-and-white alternatives that confront us today were blurred by a spectrum of intermediate positions, all of which were designed to make evolutionism seem compatible either with a liberal theology or with a secular ideology equally dedicated to the idea of progress."[18]

If contemporary sponsors of theistic evolution desire to take on board the best science, then the nonprogressivist version of Darwinism must be taken seriously.

Let us turn to the second chapter in the story of theistic evolution, the contemporary chapter. What does the loose collection of theologies we can label "theistic evolution" look like? Within contemporary theistic evolution we can find *minimalists* and *maximalists*. Minimalists are those who reluctantly find they must affirm the scientific veracity of evolutionary theory and look for ways to reconcile this branch of science with the Christian understanding of the world. Minimalists are not compelled to embrace the doctrine of progress. In fact, they tend to retain the doctrine of original sin and the realism that human beings show no capacity for moral or spiritual advancement. Other theologians are maximalists. For the maximalists, evolutionary theory provides a grand and inspiring vision of earth's epic story of the progress of life that began with inanimate matter, is now passing through our intellectual stage, and leading to still higher forms of evolutionary development toward a final spiritual achievement. Despite its demise in science, progress lives on in the work of some maximalist proponents of theistic evolution.

The following table summarizes the positions we have discussed up to this point. In each case, we have listed the attitudes toward science in general, toward biological evolution as science in particular, and toward the ideology that is associated by some with the biological model.

	Science in General	Evolutionary Science	Evolutionary Ideology
Darwinian Science	Yes	Yes	Not Necessarily
Darwinian Ideology	Yes	Yes	Yes
Scientific Creationism	Yes	No	No
Intelligent Design	Yes	No	No
Judaism	Yes	Yes	Not Necessarily
Westernized Islam	Yes	Yes	No
Theistic Evolution	Yes	Yes	No (progress?)

Let us mention two episodes in the story of theistic evolution, one minimalist Protestant and the other maximalist Roman Catholic. First, the challenge of evolution taken up within Protestantism was most intense at Princeton University and Seminary. In 1874 theologian Charles Hodge wrote an analysis of evolutionary theory, *What Is Darwinism?* Although earlier in his career he had claimed that science and religion are "the twin daughters of heaven," in this book he criticized *Origin's* exclusive reliance upon natural selection, concluding that "Darwinism is atheism." In curious contrast, Hodge's president at Princeton, James McCosh, came to almost the opposite conclusion. After an intellectual struggle, McCosh came to affirm the scientific veracity of evolutionary theory and asserted that "legitimate evolution supports Christianity."

Hodge's influential successor at Princeton was B. B. Warfield, who provided American fundamentalists with their doctrine of scriptural inspiration. What is widely overlooked is that Warfield was also a supporter of the Darwinian model of natural selection. He saw God's work in bringing the human race into existence through evolution as a parallel to the way the Holy Spirit inspired the writers of the New Testament. In fact, a significant minority of the early fundamentalists prior to the 1920s were theistic evolutionists. What historians frequently forget is that the original Christian fundamentalism did not find itself opposed to science in general or to evolution in particular; the enemy of fundamentalism was liberal Protestantism. In the first decades prior to the fundamentalist-modernist controversy of the 1920s, fundamentalists could also be Darwinists. In sum, Princeton in the late nineteenth century became the agora for theological controversy over Darwin's theory; and some theologians emerged from this discussion affirming that evolution and the Christian faith are at least compatible if not complementary.[19]

Turning to the Roman Catholics, an early twentieth-century theistic evolutionist was Pierre Teilhard de Chardin. He was the Jesuit priest and paleontologist known for discovering Peking man in 1929. Teilhard combined Darwinian evolution with the Christian doctrines of creation and redemption, creating a model of world history over deep time that traces the development of life from inanimate matter up through sentient beings into intellectual and spiritual achievements. Teilhard also projected a future in which independent human intelligences will unite with one another in a grand mystical union. Our minds will become attuned to one another's minds, and with God. "Evolution has a direction," he claimed.[20] The direction is determined by a Christ-principle now built into biological and intellectual evolution, a principle that is leading all things toward a consummate unity with God.

> Christ, principle of universal vitality because sprung up as man among men, put himself in the position . . . to purify, to direct and superanimate the general ascent of consciousness into which he inserted himself. By a personal act of communion and sublimation, he aggregates to himself the total psychism of the earth.

This is leading all consciousness toward "God, the Center of centers" at Point Omega, the culmination of the grand history of evolution.[21] Teilhard, who died in 1955, may have been the most comprehensive of the theistic evolutionists to date. Teilhard's vision is optimistic and awe inspiring. Yet, we ask: just how realistic is it?

Maximalists such as Teilhard invest a great deal of Christian capital in the doctrine of progress. The result is that the doctrine of sin becomes minimalized. All that is needed to overcome sin along with suffering, death, and evil is more time—more time to evolve. Is there good reason—either theological or scientific—to predict this kind of transformed future? If nature "red in tooth and claw" is what we have inherited from our evolutionary past, what might provide sufficient reason to believe tomorrow will be better than yesterday or today?

In considering the merits of a constructive theistic evolution, we listen carefully to what Bowler says.

> The very fact that Christianity takes such a pessimistic view of the human situation makes it the best-placed of all the major religions to deal with the challenges of Darwinism. For those Christians who can face the prospect of breaking with a literal interpretation of Genesis, the

fact that evolution does not seem to be focused on progress and preordained purpose offers a chance to explore the possibility of a creative synthesis with modern biology.[22]

THEISTIC EVOLUTION ACCORDING TO MARTY AND TED

We the authors of this introduction to Darwin's *Origin*, Marty and Ted, place ourselves in the theistic evolution camp somewhere between Princeton and Teilhard. We cannot endorse everything said by every other theistic evolutionist, to be sure. In addition, we would like to attend to the stricter version of the Darwinian model, the nonprogressive version that methodologically blinds itself to design or purpose built-in to nature. Still, we affirm that through the long story of life's evolution God has been at work and will continue to be at work in creating and redeeming a world God loves. In what follows we would like to share with you some key planks in a theistic evolution platform, one that unites strategies of evolutionary science with the Christian vision of creation and redemption.

Here we propose seven principles of theistic evolution. We offer them as hypotheses, as proposals for consideration. They provide illumination, though something less than the brightness of final truth. Borrowing from science, our principles make up a "theological model" that we hope will shed light on further reflection as well as provide spiritual guidance.

First, we recommend that *the Darwinian model of evolution should be conditionally accepted*, even by religious persons. We accept and work with the Darwinian model as we would any other scientific theory—that is, if it's explanatory for observed data and if it's fertile for the growth of new knowledge, then it is worth embracing for the time being. No scientific theory is eternal. Nor is it apodictally true. Eventually, all theories get replaced with better ones. The Darwinian model is today's best science. Scientific creationism and ID provide only inferior science, perhaps not even science at all.

By the Darwinian model we mean its fertile scientific core, not the ideological layers that bury the science. Although it is tempting to deal with the layers of ideology, we have made strenuous attempts to drill beneath in order to gain the most fertile understanding of the natural world. Attending to the layers of ideology could be diversionary. We do not want to provide theological baptism for epistemological or ontological reductionism, for progress, for social Darwinism or eugenics, let alone atheistic materialism. It is understandable why some theistic evolutionists are tempted to incorporate the doctrine of progress; yet we caution ourselves to avoid this. As we formulate our own variant of theistic evolution, we do so in light of God's promise for a new creation without incorporating the idea of progress into our understanding of nature.

Second, we think of God's action in nature's world this way: *God is the primary cause while nature operates according to secondary causes.* As the primary cause, God is the creator of all things. God brought the world into existence from nothing. And God continues to sustain the world in its existence. Within the created order, the world operates according to laws and principles. Events are contingent and sometimes free—that is, what happens in nature and in human life is unpredictable. Yet much that happens is the result of secondary causes, the result of one natural creature relating to another natural creature. Science studies the realm of secondary causation, not primary causation.

We would like to add that primary causation does not imply a vague deism, an uninvolved sustaining of the world's existence. God may also act providentially, caring for the world. Yet such providential divine action complements without upsetting the nexus of secondary causation. Robert John Russell, to illustrate, says *"we can now understand special providence as the objective acts of God in nature and history and we can understand these acts in a noninterventionist manner consistent with science."*[23] Science can discern the laws that govern natural processes and observe those very processes; but science cannot on its own perceive the source of those laws nor divine action within those processes.

Third, we need to attend to the question of purpose. So we offer this: *God has a purpose for nature that scientists cannot see within nature.* We do not expect a research scientist looking through the lenses of random variation and natural selection to perceive a grand design in nature or an inherent purpose toward which all things are moving. As both ID supporters and evolutionary biologists acknowledge, some systems in nature exhibit characteristics of design. The eye, for example, is designed for seeing. Yet local design in complex systems does not in itself give evidence of a single grand design for the totality of the created universe. As Christians, we believe the entire created universe has a purpose, a divinely appointed purpose. To discern that purpose we will need to rely on a special revelation from God.

Fourth, we need to bridge God's purpose with what happens in nature. So we offer this: *God's promised new creation provides the purpose for the present creation.* We rely on three important passages from Scripture. First, Genesis 1:31, "God saw everything that he had made, and indeed, it was very good." Second, Revelation 21:1, "Then I saw a new heaven and a new earth." Third, between these two, we live with St. Paul who writes in 1 Corinthians 13:12, "now we see in a mirror, dimly." We are cautious, because we can only see dimly in a mirror that reflects back what we project into it. Because science cannot shine light on the new creation promised by the Bible, we can apprehend it only in faith and trust.

Fifth, we offer an ontological principle: *God creates from the future, not from the past.* We believe that God creates the world by giving it a future. This is what God did at the beginning, in Genesis 1:1–2:4a. For God to say that this world is "very good," God must already have had in mind the anticipated new creation prophesied in Revelation 21 and 22. This will be the redeemed creation. It will be the creation where all illnesses will be healed, where there will be no crying or pain, and where death shall be no more. Further, it will be the creation where the lion will lie down with the lamb, and we the human race will live in harmony with all of nature. Only when the created world has attained this redeemed state will it finally be created and dubbed "very good."

Sixth, when it comes to interpreting the Bible, we offer this: *the book of Genesis does not describe a finished event in the past; rather, it describes the full sweep of God's creative activities that includes us today.* The account of creation in Genesis 1:1–2:4a, we believe, applies to the entire history of the cosmos, beginning perhaps with the Big Bang 13.7 billion years ago and extending into the future far enough to take into account the advent of the new creation the Bible promises. Right now, God is at work. God is working as primary cause with all of nature's secondary causes—natural causes as understood by physicists, chemists, biologists, geneticists, and neuroscientists—to bring into existence an ever-more-complex realm of interaction between ourselves, our world, and our God. We today find ourselves somewhere between day one and day six. Day seven, the Sabbath, is scheduled for the day after the arrival of the prophesied New Jerusalem of the closing chapters of the Bible. Then God can declare that all of creation is "very good" and take that well-deserved divine rest.

Seventh, we suggest that *redemption coincides with creation.* One of the mistakes of both the creationists and the ID supporters is to limit the theological questions posed to science to the domain of creation (even though, as we saw, Henry Morris would like to interpret creation christo-logically). We believe creation cannot be understood from the perspec-tive of faith unless it is viewed in light of redemption. So, even if creationism or ID should be successful at unseating the Darwinian model, it would not follow that the distinctively Christian viewpoint will have prevailed. What is distinctively Christian is not an explanation for a bio-logical world replete with extinctions, predator-prey violence, suffering from disease, and falling by the wayside while only the reproductively fit survive. Rather, what is distinctively Christian is reliance upon Isaiah's prophecy that in God's kingdom the lion will lie down with the lamb and all of the creation will live in harmony. Without this transformative vision, we cannot deal adequately with God's relation to the creation; and we cannot understand clearly where science can be of help or not be of help in articulating our faith in God.

Does this mean we are buying into the ideology of progress? No. We do not conflate evolution with progress. We do not buy this ideology, or any of the other Darwinian ideologies. We do not want to Christianize Darwinian progressivism. Rather, we assess the Darwinian model from the standpoint of the divine promise of a new creation. We believe that God's creative work is not done yet. We anticipate its furtherance and its consummate fulfillment.

THREE THEOLOGIES OF EVOLUTION: A COMPARISON

At the beginning of the twenty-first century, the initial theological questions and concerns Darwin had to confront persisted in almost their nineteenth-century form. Like trees belonging to a forest, all refer us to the larger question: is it satisfactory to provide naturalistic explanations for evolution that leave God out of the scientific picture? Some theolo-gians are satisfied with restricting scientific explanations to secondary causation. Others, quite unsatisfied with the removal of God from the picture of evolution, are seeking explanations for natural processes that include direct divine causation. Theologians ask: does God intervene in the natural world? If so, when and how and for what purpose?

In the current evolution controversy, as we have just seen, voices from three distinctive schools of theological thinking can be heard: (1) cre-ationism, (2) intelligent design, and (3) theistic evolution. These three can be heard filing complaints against atheism, especially when atheists claim to base their antitheology on the science of evolution.

Before we compare and contrast these alternatives, let us remind ourselves of the distinction between *methodological reductionism* and *ontological reductionism*. Reductionism is a principle of scientific research: natural phenomena at one level should be explained by the laws of the lower level. For example, biological phenomena should be explained by chemistry. Chemical phenomena should be explained by physics. Or, to say it another way, what appears to us as a whole phenomenon should be explained by the parts that make it up. A scientist feels he or she understands a phenomenon when it is explained by the parts that make it up. By way of contrast to such a reductionist approach, explaining the parts in light of the whole would constitute an emergentist approach.

Methodological reductionism is a conceptual research tool that sets the parameters for arriving at explanations. By seeking reductionist explanations for discrete phenomena, the research scientist is not making claims about the whole of reality. The scope of scientific claims is limited to the phenomenon under examination, limited to identifying only the natural causes at work.

Ontological reductionists wish to say much more. They contend that all of reality can be reduced to the single nexus of physical causes. Nature is all there is. Nothing supranatural exists. No God, no spiritual entities exist. Scientific explanations are the only explanations that constitute human knowledge. Religious claims regarding supranatural things are judged to be mere fictions. They do not constitute knowledge of reality. There is only one reality, nature, and science is nature's prophet. Ontological reductionism constitutes an antireligious ideology placed on top of science. It dons tee shirts with many labels: atheism, materialism, or secular humanism.

All theologies of evolution reject ontological reductionism. Theologians are divided on the question of methodological reductionism, however. Some theologians reject methodological reductionism, while others affirm it. Some schools of theology believe God's actions in the natural world are discernable—that is, if our scientific glasses have been cleaned, then we can plainly see the design and purpose of God at work within natural phenomena. Other theologians, who accept methodological reductionism within the limits of science, appeal to special revelation instead of science to discern the presence of God in the created world. Science and faith are complements, according to the theistic evolutionists. The creationists and intelligent design advocates are reluctant to accept methodological reductionism, whereas the theistic evolutionists are at peace with it. All three groups repudiate ontological reductionism with its accompanying atheism.

The following figure (3.1) presents the various positions as part of a spectrum of divine action, from complete interventionism to complete noninterventionism.

We may look at these differences another way. We can compare these schools of thought on the question of divine intervention into the causal nexus of the natural realm. Creationists are interventionists, claiming that God created not just the world but also each individual species at the world's genesis. God, according to the creationists, is responsible for the form that each species takes. Speciation is not due to a lengthy, gradual evolution.

Intelligent design advocates, in partial contrast, accept that speciation has taken place over deep time. But, they add, advances to higher levels of complexity (complex emergent wholes greater than the sum of their parts) require the direct causal action of an intelligent designer—a transcendent

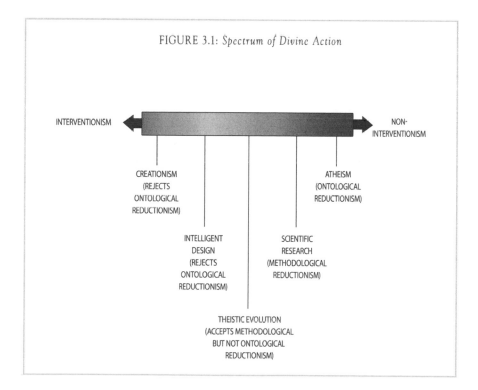

FIGURE 3.1: *Spectrum of Divine Action*

INTERVENTIONISM

NON-INTERVENTIONISM

CREATIONISM
(REJECTS
ONTOLOGICAL
REDUCTIONISM)

ATHEISM
(ONTOLOGICAL
REDUCTIONISM)

INTELLIGENT
DESIGN
(REJECTS
ONTOLOGICAL
REDUCTIONISM)

SCIENTIFIC
RESEARCH
(METHODOLOGICAL
REDUCTIONISM)

THEISTIC EVOLUTION
(ACCEPTS METHODOLOGICAL
BUT NOT ONTOLOGICAL
REDUCTIONISM)

designer. Appeal to natural causes alone provides an insufficient explanation. These two schools of thought describe interventionist divine action as one cause among others within the natural nexus.

The theistic evolutionists, in contrast to both the creationists and ID advocates, affirm indirect divine action, not direct. God acts in the world as primary cause—as the world's creator—but the world of nature evolves over time according to the laws of secondary causation. Saying it still another way, proponents of creationism and intelligent design rely on a miraculous understanding of divine action; whereas theistic evolutionists seek a nonmiraculous understanding of God's action through natural law. Theistic evolutionists are free to affirm occasional miracles as exceptions to natural laws, of course; but day-to-day natural phenomena must obey the natural laws that reductionist scientists can discover and rely upon for their explanations.

Before leaving this chapter, please note the line on the spectrum indicating "scientific research." Marty, one of the coauthors of this chapter, is a professional scientist. In a lengthy career at a university with a medical school, he has investigated viruses in his laboratory. He has coauthored three editions of a textbook on virology.[24] He knows from extensive experience that good science requires methodological reductionism. He finds Darwin's theory of evolution indispensable for learning more about molecular biology and producing the kind of scientific knowledge that could lead to advances in medical therapy. Still, Marty wants no part of ontological materialism, let alone atheism. He wants good science, and good science alone. Science at its best recognizes the limits of its frame of reference. It recognizes that its legitimacy is limited to the domain of naturalistic explanations. Science has no right to make claims about the existence or nonexistence of God, let alone whether we can see traces of divine grace and beauty exhibited by the natural world.

CHAPTER FOUR

SCIENTIFIC CONCEPTS:
THEN AND NOW

Although Darwin was writing 150 years before the current scientific age, many of the key concepts with which he worked are still important in biology. Some have remained much the same as they were in his day, and others have changed drastically. In this chapter, we will provide a guided tour through a few of these, taking a look at what Darwin understood and where we are now.

In each case, we will lead you through some of the material from *Origin of Species* that bears on the concept. In some cases, this will be selected from a large set, in others, one or two statements will be all that there is. We will then try to frame this in terms of the present-day understanding of the concept.

In all of these examples, we are not only focusing on the details of the concept but also on how the science of the theory of evolution, the model that Darwin proposed, has both explanatory power and fruitfulness. We want to emphasize one of our main points: people of faith need to embrace good science. Darwin's model has proved to be good science, because it is still fertile and still generating progressive research. This is the main reason that religious people need to respect it and take it seriously.

In this chapter, we will briefly discuss seven of these scientific concepts. Because of the contemporary importance of the matter of design in nature, we will reserve an additional chapter for the design issue.

WHAT DOES "SPECIES" MEAN?

The title of Darwin's *magnum opus* is *Origin of Species*. So we might ask: just what is a species? The answer is not a simple one. At the present time in the history of biology there are three conceptual definitions of "species."[1]:

1. The *reproductive isolation concept* reigns in the field of today's biology. If two populations of organisms cannot mate and produce fertile offspring, they are said to be reproductively isolated. Therefore, they constitute separate biological species.
2. The *phylogenetic species concept* is defined with respect to a common ancestor. According to this criterion, species are identified as the terminal points of a phylogenetic tree.
3. The *morphospecies concept* is used for fossil remains. In this case, anatomical differences and similarities of the fossil bones and other structures are used to make the definition of species.

What does all of this mean? Well, certainly Darwin did not have this array of definitions in mind when he agreed to entitle his book *Origin of Species*. Instead he tried to use only the first of these—the biological species concept. For instance, he quotes the work of Benjamin Walsh, an Englishman who had emigrated to the United States and eventually served as the first state entomologist for Illinois. Walsh was studying insects that feed on plants (phytophagic insects) and, in 1863, articulated a definition for species versus varieties. Darwin quoted him in the fourth and subsequent editions of *Origin*:

> But no observer can determine for another, even if he can do so for himself, which of these Phytophagic forms ought to be called species and which varieties. Mr. Walsh ranks the forms which it may be supposed would freely intercross, as varieties; and those which appear to have lost this power, as species.[2]

Of course, Linnaeus had something in mind when he proposed "species" as the lowest level of organization to be used in his system of classification. However, he did not mean this term in the same sense as Darwin did. His concept was that species, which defined specific organisms, were unchanging over time. In this sense of the term it refers more to a "type" or kind of object with shared properties. His binomial nomenclature (genus/species, for instance, *Homo sapiens*), did bring order to chaos in biology, but it did not offer a specific meaning for the term, other than as a collection of individuals that share some defining properties, making their group unique.

Clearly, Darwin considered reproductive isolation as a species-defining concept, especially in his early writings.[3] However, by the time he finished the first edition of *Origin of Species*, he was less clear about this. Although he quoted Walsh, above, he then mixed his ideas about varieties and species throughout. Thus, by the sixth edition, we still do not have a definitive statement of what he really meant by "species."

The biological species concept was most clearly proclaimed in the modern era by Ernst Mayr. A few years before his passing, he reviewed the status of this concept in a marvelous essay, written for the journal *Philosophy of Science*. In this paper, he restated his basic definition, originally published in 1969:

> The segregation of the total genetic variability of nature into discrete packages, so called species, which are separated from each other by reproductive barriers, prevents the production of too great a number of disharmonious incompatible gene combinations. This is the basic biological meaning of species.[4]

Or, as Mayr put it more simply in the 1996 paper, "Species are groups of interbreeding natural populations that are reproductively isolated from other such groups."

With the dominance of the molecular paradigm in biology in the latter part of the twentieth century it was only natural that the idea of reproductive isolation came to mean the restriction of gene flow. This can be seen in the discussion given in a textbook on evolution, published in 2004:

> Reproductive isolation is clearly an appropriate criterion for identifying species because it confirms the lack of gene flow. This is the litmus test of evolutionary independence in organisms that reproduce sexually.[5]

However, this reliance on the molecular nature of information in biology is being challenged by the observation that horizontal gene transfer (HGT) may be more common than originally thought.[6] HGT involves the movement of DNA (genes) from one organism to another in the same generation. This is quite common among bacteria but was not known to occur in higher forms of cells, especially in eukaryotic cells that make up all of the rest of life. However, as Goldenfeld and Woese argue, this might have been a common feature of early forms of life, resulting in a possible blurring of the species definition if it relies solely upon information flow.

Ernst Mayr recognized this potential problem and recast his definition of the mechanism of reproductive isolation as the "biological properties of individuals which prevent the interbreeding (fusion) of populations."[7] Notice that his new statement relies on whole organisms and populations. One could say that it is not reductionistic, but rather wholistic. This is indeed interesting, given that biology is going through a revolutionary period that will see the end of reductionism as an epistemological, if not ontological, philosophical position.

THE CLASSIFICATION OF LIVING THINGS

It is perhaps obvious that Darwin, in order to arrive at his model, had to have some idea of the classification schemes for living things. Not only did he have to be familiar with the most current organization, but he also had to be reasonably adept at observation and taxonomic details. No one biologist could be expected to be expert in all organisms, not even in Darwin's time. So it was that he had to wait until he returned to London after his time on the Beagle to collaborate with other naturalists in order to examine his collected materials. For instance, all of the zoological findings from his voyage were published under Darwin's editorship (the works all say "edited and superintended by Charles Darwin"), but were written with Richard Owen (mammals), George Waterhouse (mammals), John Gould (birds), Leonard Jenyns (fish), and Thomas Bell (reptiles).[8] The most problematic of these collaborators turned out to be Owen, who, in later years, turned against Darwin and his theory of evolution.

Over the decades, and now more than a century and a half, since Darwin returned from his voyage, the science of biological classification has changed with the addition of more sophisticated tools, although the aim is still the same.

Darwin's conclusion was that by careful classification and comparative taxonomy, one could reason that all currently living species descended from a common ancestor. In his view of the planet's history over deep time, this would entail a "tree of life" image. In fact, the only figure that Darwin included in *Origin of Species* was just such a tree, showing his theoretical argument for speciation and extinction events, leading to the species we currently observe. Figure 4.1 is a reproduction of that figure:

Modern biologists have not deviated a great deal from this kind of thinking. In an introductory textbook of evolution, "tree-thinking" is introduced at the outset, with reference to Darwin's diagram:

FIGURE 4.1: *Darwin's Tree of Life*

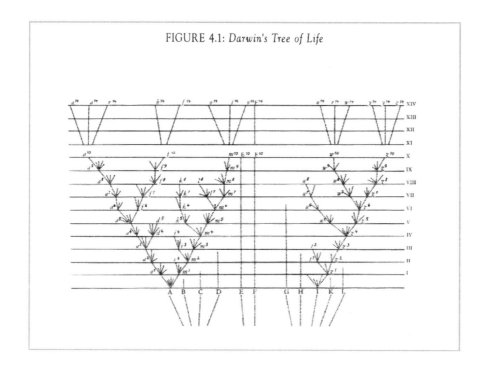

In creating this diagram, Darwin invented a technique for illustrating how species are related by descent with modification from a common ancestor. The evolutionary trees, or phylogenies, published in today's scientific literature are the direct descendants of Darwin's graphical device.[9]

Modern tree of life diagrams can readily be found in the current literature. A recent publication in *Science* has one that is an attempt to represent phylogenetic relationship using genomic data, and is called a global tree.[10] Although drawn in a circular format, the graphic device is, as Freeman and Herron suggest, a direct descendant of Darwin's original figure.

GENETICS AND INHERITANCE

Darwin, as a scientist of the middle to late nineteenth century, had a limited understanding of the nature of inheritance. At that time, it was thought that the traits of the parents were somehow "blended" into the offspring. As we have seen, this became one of the most severe scientific critiques of Darwin's model. After all, how could natural selection work if traits could ultimately be diluted by blending?

Mendel's work, unrecognized in the nineteenth century, would come to be a key feature of the modern or neo-Darwinian synthesis of the twentieth century. Indeed, it is fair to say that the search for the nature of the gene, which the rediscovery of Mendel precipitated, has changed evolutionary biology in dramatic ways. Modern phylogenetic trees of life are constructed entirely from considerations of comparative genomics. No classic taxonomy in used in their formulation.

With the advent of rapid techniques for large-scale analysis of informational molecules such as nucleic acids and proteins, the age of genomics has blossomed into being. It would be more accurate to call this the age of bioinformatics, since biologists routinely analyze the DNA component of an organism (genomics), along with the products of the genes encoded in the DNA (proteomics). In addition, the interactions of these proteins can be analyzed and used to predict the network status of a particular cell (the interactome). However, it has been the very tools and accumulated data of this new age that have brought the concept of the gene to its virtual knees.

The Human Genome Project (HGP) from 1990 to 2003 was initially seen as the first "big science" undertaking of biology. The history of the HGP is entangled with that of the Manhattan Project, the Atomic Energy Commission (now the Nuclear Regulatory Commission), and the Department of Energy (DOE). At the end of World War II, there was great interest in the biological effects of radiation. Much of the early work was in concert with Japanese researchers and focused on survivors of the Hiroshima and Nagasaki blasts. The Atomic Bomb Casualty Commission was charged with this effort, and was continually looking for more refined analytical tools to examine the human genome. What more refined tool could there be than determining the nucleotide sequence of the genes?

And so, with funding from DOE, and ultimately in collaboration with the National Institutes of Health (NIH), the grand quest for the sequence of all human genes was envisioned in 1986. A number of websites devoted to the HGP are available, with the history of the project covered in reasonable detail (except for the Manhattan Project connection) on a site maintained by the DOE.[11]

With important modifications of approach and the development of even more rapid tools, the goal of sequencing the regions of the human chromosome set that express products was achieved ahead of schedule and announced in early 2001.[12] The analysis of the data then began. It had been predicted that humans would have more than one hundred thousand genes. To the shock of many, when the massive data set was analyzed, it turns out that we have on the order of twenty to twenty-five thousand genes. Not only is this many fewer than expected, but what happens in the human genome is also not much different than what we find in the fruit fly. In addition to this, the data revealed that the definition of a gene is no longer so clear. As a result, biology has been dramatically turned on its ear. The reductionist paradigm has run its course and it is now time for a new approach, one that is more fruitful and has greater explanatory power. The direction followed now is toward a systems view, a more holistic understanding of the molecular nature of life.[13] We will discuss this in more detail below.

VARIATION AND MUTATION

A central feature of the evolutionary model is that within any population individual members can exhibit variation. A great deal of *Origin of Species* is occupied with the description of inherited variations. In fact, three chapters (1, 2, and 5) are devoted specifically to the occurrence and nature of variation.

Chapter 5 of *Origin* is entitled "Laws of Variation." The contents of the chapter are far from that. As Darwin wrote in his summary of this section:

> Our ignorance of the laws of variation is profound. Not in one case out of a hundred can we pretend to assign any reason why this or that part differs, more or less, from the same part in the parents.[14]

This "profound ignorance" was, of course, due to the fact that naturalists of the late nineteenth century had no idea how inheritance operates, let alone any concept of something like a gene. Nevertheless, Darwin and others were aware that variations occur within populations and that they are inherited. It is the gradual accumulation of such variations, over deep time and under the influence of natural selection, that ultimately leads to speciation.

With the advent of the age of Mendelian genetics at the beginning of the twentieth century, the idea of the gene as the repository of inherited information took hold. The search for the nature of the gene ultimately led to an understanding of the nature of DNA and to the discovery of the mechanisms by which changes in this molecule lead to changes in that information. Such changes are called mutations.

A mutation is defined as a stable, inheritable change in the DNA base sequence that specifies the information content of the genes or in their controlling sequence regions. A common misunderstanding of mutations is that they are all deleterious. On the contrary, most mutations ultimately have no effect. This is because cells have evolved protective mechanisms that tend to ensure the integrity of the genetic information. In fact, DNA replication, the cellular event that produces the genetic information for the next generation, has an overall fidelity of about one mistake in every ten billion DNA subunits (bases) copied.

Mutations can occur spontaneously, due to the chemistry of the molecules of information. In addition, mutations can take place as a result of ionizing radiation or because of the presence of certain chemicals in the environment. All three of these causes combine to produce a given rate of mutation for living things on this planet.

There are three consequences of mutational events: neutral, deleterious, or beneficial. It is the relative frequency of each of these events that is the topic of disagreement. Clearly, the evolutionary model requires that some mutational events confer a selective advantage on the organism. Such a mutation might be called beneficial. On the other hand, a deleterious mutation, say, one leading to a loss of function for a gene, would not confer a selective advantage, at least not at first glance. Finally, neutral mutations are events that do not change the function of a gene, or, more broadly, do not influence the selective advantage of a gene, even if they do change the function in some way.

It has been proposed that the vast majority of mutation events fall into the neutral category. While this is still hotly debated, the idea that only a small fraction of mutational events are deleterious is generally accepted and flies in the face of the notion that mutations are, per se, bad. The so-called neutral mutation theory, proposed first by Motoo Kimura in 1968, argues that most mutational events have no Darwinian effect and are therefore selectively opaque. Another, perhaps more controversial, view of mutation is the adaptive mutation model, wherein a selective pressure decreases the deleterious mutations and influences the beneficial mutations in a direction that is driven by or relieves the pressure. In some sense, this is a model that incorporates a modern version of a doctrine of progress, which we have discussed in previous chapters.

However we view the nature and value of mutational changes, the net result is the occurrence of variations within a population. In the long view of evolutionary history, it is this pool of variations upon which natural selection acts. At present we recognize the molecular nature of variation as differences in the genetic information that is encoded in the genome, or even as the differences in expressed products of that genome at the protein level. How these differences translate into the large-scale level variations that Darwin and his contemporaries observed is often not entirely worked out.

One modern analysis of variations is a direct outcome of the HGP. The very rapid and highly specific techniques developed to accomplish this massive undertaking have given scientists the ability to examine the human genome for very slight variations on a population level. Using a technique called *haplotype mapping* that finds specific regions of DNA where a single bit of information might vary in human samples (*single nucleotide polymorphisms*, or SNPs), a map of these population-level variations has been generated.[15] These slight variations make up only about a tenth of a percent of the human genome and, as result, mean that we are really all the same.

However, the variations, or at least the pattern of variation, can, in some cases, be correlated with medical data. So it is that the positive goal of studying the HapMap is to customize medical delivery to subpopulations, providing improved health care. An unfortunate fallout from this analysis, however, is the resurgence of racial distinctions, at least in the view of some. It turns out that these population variations have been most often grouped by ethnic identifiers. Thus, people speak of the African American HapMap or the Chinese HapMap. While the genomic differences that are referenced are so slight as to be inconsequential, the problem is that racial or ethnic distinctions have the potential to become reified in genomic sequence. Troy Duster has commented on the negative aspects of this latest HGP effort. He argues that the racial designations of the subpopulations are flawed, to say the least. As a result, the use of these data tends to commit the Whiteheadian "fallacy of misplaced concreteness" or the "fallacy of reification." Duster concludes:

> If we fall into the trap of accepting the (racial) categories of stored data sets, then it can be an easy slide down the slope to the misconceptions of "black" or "white" diseases. By accepting the prefabricated racial designations of stored samples and then reporting patterns of differences in SNPs between those categories, misplaced genetic concreteness is nearly inevitable.[16]

As we write this chapter the specter of racial identification with genetics raises its head once more, this time in the person of James Watson, the Nobel laureate of DNA fame. In an interview with the *Sunday Times* of London, Watson was quoted by interviewer Charlotte Hunte-Grubbe about his ideas on intelligence and race. The full text from that article follows:

> He says that he is "inherently gloomy about the prospect of Africa" because "all our social policies are based on the fact that their intelligence is the same as ours—whereas all the testing says not really," and I know that this "hot potato" is going to be difficult to address. His hope is that everyone is equal, but he counters that "people who have to deal with black employees find this not true." He says that you should not discriminate on the basis of colour, because "there are many people of colour who are very talented, but don't promote them when they haven't succeeded at the lower level." He writes that "there is no firm reason to anticipate that the intellectual capacities of peoples geographically separated in their evolution should prove to have evolved identically. Our wanting to reserve equal powers of reason as some universal heritage of humanity will not be enough to make it so."[17]

Clearly the issue that Duster raises is still with us—the racial paradigm enshrined in the evolutionary model is alive and well.

SURVIVAL OF THE FITTEST: WHAT IS MEANT BY REPRODUCTIVE ADVANTAGE?

Competition was implicit in Darwin's model. In fact, one of the key elements of *Origin of Species* is the acknowledgement of the Malthusian model of population. In order for natural selection to affect the progress of a population, selective conditions have to exist. Darwin realized that this would be the case for a population that outreproduced the ability of the resources to support it.

Thomas Robert Malthus was a British economist, demographer, and ordained Anglican minister whose influential book, *An Essay on the Principle of Population*, was published in 1798. Malthus argued that, if left unchecked, a population would increase geometrically (increasing by a percentage of the total), while the resources to support this population would only increase arithmetically (increasing by the addition of a fixed amount). As a result, he predicted that the population would soon outstrip the ability of the environment to support it.

Darwin was greatly influenced by this proposal. He assumed that natural populations would obey this model and that, because of this prediction, more individuals would be born than could survive. Darwin introduces this concept at the very beginning. In chapter 3 of *Origin* ("Struggle for Existence"), he elaborates on its meaning:

A struggle for existence inevitably follows from the high rate at which all organic beings tend to increase. Every being, which during its natural lifetime produces several eggs or seeds, must suffer destruction during some period of its life, and during some season or occasional year, otherwise, on the principle of geometrical increase, its numbers would quickly become so inordinately great that no country could support the product. Hence, as more individuals are produced than can possibly survive, there must in every case be a struggle for existence, either one individual with another of the same species, or with the individuals of distinct species, or with the physical conditions of life. It is the doctrine of Malthus applied with manifold force to the whole animal and vegetable kingdoms; for in this case there can be no artificial increase of food, and no prudential restraint from marriage.[18]

Given this, Darwin argued that any variation present in the population that tended to enhance the advantage that an individual might have would result in a greater representation of that variation in the resulting population. Notice that what Darwin is really talking about here is the advantage that results in the greater chance for reproduction, and their offspring more represented in subsequent population distributions. He states this throughout *Origin of Species*, and, in the last chapter ("Recapitulation and Conclusion") he summarizes this argument:

As each species tends by its geometrical rate of reproduction to increase inordinately in number; and as the modified descendants of each species will be enabled to increase by as much as they become more diversified in habits and structure, so as to be able to seize on many and widely different places in the economy of nature, there will be a constant tendency in natural selection to preserve the most divergent offspring of any one species.[19]

Darwin termed this "the struggle for existence." However, Herbert Spencer had the final word. Spencer, the great English philosopher and naturalist of late nineteenth-century England, was somewhat of a competitor early on for Darwin. Spencer had, after all, written about an evolutionary model before the publication of *Origin of Species*. However, with the publication of Darwin's book, the two became a mutual admiration society. Spencer read the book and became an instant fan. In his own book, *Principles of Biology*, he quotes extensively from *Origin of Species*. It is in this work of Spencer's that the phrase "survival of the fittest" first appears:

> This survival of the fittest, which I have here sought to express in mechanical terms, is that which Mr. Darwin has called "natural selection, or the preservation of favoured races in the struggle for life." That there goes on a process of this kind throughout the organic world, Mr. Darwin's great work on the Origin of Species has shown to the satisfaction of nearly all naturalists.[20]

Not to be outdone, Darwin picks up this phrase and inserts it into the fifth and subsequent editions of *Origin of Species*:

> I have called this principle, by which each slight variation, if useful, is preserved, by the term natural selection, in order to mark its relation to man's power of selection. But the expression often used by Mr. Herbert Spencer, of the Survival of the Fittest, is more accurate, and is sometimes equally convenient.[21]

Thus, we have inherited the abiding image of the evolutionary model that is so well captured in this phrase. In fact, we often couple "survival of the fittest" with the line "nature red in tooth and claw." Of course, this is from an epic poem by Alfred, Lord Tennyson, *In Memoriam A.H.H.* This work, written to commemorate the death of Lord Tennyson's friend, was completed in 1849, ten years before the publication of *Origin of Species*. The line is found in Canto 56 of the poem:

> Who trusted God was love indeed
> And love Creation's final law—
> Tho' Nature, red in tooth and claw
> With ravine, shriek'd against his creed—[22]

Tennyson did not have Darwin's model in mind when he wrote this. Nevertheless, the line evokes the flavor of Spencer's coinage and remains one of the most powerful images associated with biological evolution.

The competition implied in Darwin's original work was a hallmark of evolutionary thought well into the twentieth century. Reproductive advantage meant that the offspring of a variant would ultimately "outgrow" those without the selectable modification. This was not only witnessed in the historical biological record, but also observed in such "experiments" as the famous peppered moth study in England.[23]

However, today more emphasis is being placed on cooperative models as opposed to competition. With the advent of network science approaches in biology, discussed below, it is likely that we will see examples of interactive properties that lead to selective advantage for both organisms.

ONTOGENY / PHYLOGENY: A FLAWED COMPARISON?

In chapter 14 ("Mutual Affinities of Organic Beings") of *Origin of Species*, Darwin discusses embryology and the early developmental stages of organisms. He makes reference in this section to the work of two contemporaries: Karl von Baer and Ernst Haeckel.

Karl von Baer was a noted Estonian biologist who was one of the founders of the study of early development: embryology. Before Darwin's voyage, von Baer had already (in 1828) formulated what Darwin would call the "laws for embryonic resemblance,"[24] more formally called Baer's laws of embryology. In essence, Baer stated that the embryo of a higher animal never resembles the adult form of another animal, but at earliest times might resemble the embryo of that animal. Von Baer strenuously rejected the idea that embryos transform through a linear series that was akin to classification schemes. These pre-Darwinian notions held that embryos of higher animals resembled the adults of more primitive species. Von Baer argued that, while it was true that embryos went through some common stages, they eventually differentiated from that stage and from each other. Therefore, even though human embryos at one time have what could be described as gill slits, they in no way are said to be the same as fish embryos.

Karl von Baer never accepted Darwin's model. On the other hand, Darwin relied heavily on von Baer's laws of embryology and observations to bolster his theory. The idea that homologous structures could be observed in the embryos of various species was, for Darwin, strong evidence in support of descent from a common ancestor. In chapter 14, he quotes extensively from von Baer concerning early embryos and their resemblance, wherein von Baer concludes that "'the feet of lizards and mammals, the wings and feet of birds, no less than the hands and feet of man, all arise from the same fundamental form.'"[25]

The counterargument to von Baer's ideas had appeared prior to Darwin's publication, and, in fact, continued throughout the nineteenth century. This argument was that the resemblance of embryonic forms was evidence that what Darwin would come to call the evolutionary history of life is seen in the developmental stages of higher animals. This theory was called *recapitulation*. Von Baer disagreed with this strenuously, but several noted biologists, including the great Louis Agassiz, continued to argue for this position. It fell, however, to Ernst Haeckel, the German biologist, to be the one with whom this concept would be linked.

Haeckel was also a supporter of the recapitulation model. Although he wrote extensively in both biology and philosophy, and was an important contributor to nineteenth-century German science, it was a series of embryological drawings that he made that have turned out to be his enduring legacy. In order to demonstrate what he meant, he produced the series of drawings comparing early embryos of different species, all at what is called the *tail-bud stage*. The drawings (figure 4.2) are shown here from Haeckel's original:

FIGURE 4.2: *Haeckel's Drawing Comparing Early Embryos of Different Species*

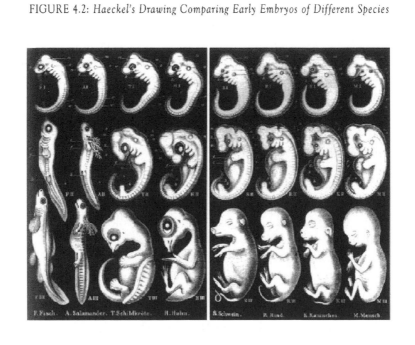

The image shows, left to right, embryos of fish, salamander, turtle, chicken, pig, cow, rabbit, and human. The top row shows his rendition of these embryos at the tail-bud stage. Haeckel concluded that all of these looked the same at the earliest stage. The recapitulation model argued that each embryo goes through morphological stages that are identical to the adult stages of lower forms. Thus, the human goes through a fish form, and so forth. Haeckel's conclusion is summed up in the phrase "ontogeny recapitulates phylogeny."

Belief that ontogeny recapitulates phylogeny became a virtually unquestioned axiom in Western science. Many science textbooks in American schools today still presume this to be fact. The idea was so protean that even the famed founder of psychoanalysis, Sigmund Freud, employed the assumption when comparing today's mental illnesses to earlier stages in human evolution.

> Prehistoric man, in the various stages of his development, is known to us through the inanimate monuments and implements which he has left behind, through the information about his art, his religion and his attitude toward life which has come to us either directly or by way of tradition handed down in legends, myths and fairy tales, and through the relics of his mode of thought which survive in our own manners and customs. But apart from this, in a certain sense he is still our contemporary. There are men still living who, as we believe, stand very near to primitive man, far nearer than we do, and whom we therefore regard as his direct heirs and representatives. Such is our view of those whom we describe as savages or half-savages; and their mental life must have a peculiar interest for us if we are right in seeing in it a well-preserved picture of an early stage of our own development.

Then, Freud continues to draw out implications.

> If that supposition is correct, a comparison between the psychology of primitive peoples, as it is taught by social anthropology, and the psychology of neurotics, as it has been revealed by psychoanalysis, will be bound to show numerous points of agreement and will throw new light upon familiar facts in both sciences.[26]

Haeckel's conclusion, and hence Freud's, turns out to be based upon a false observation, negated by detailed studies of embryological forms. In addition, it has been suggested that Haeckel embellished his drawings to emphasize the supposed similarities. The problem was that his drawings and the phrase made its way into textbooks and persisted into the twentieth century.

Haeckel's statement has been challenged over and over, most recently by Stephen Jay Gould. In addition, the embryological comparisons made in the famous drawing have been examined using modern photographic methods with a similar set of organisms. The latter set of results was published in 1997, and concluded that the tail-bud stages of fish, amphibians, reptiles, birds, and mammals are all vastly different morphologically.[27] This paper, along with others, has finally put to rest the value of Haeckel's nineteenth-century drawing.

However, it was Stephen Jay Gould who took this topic on as an historical investigation in one of his earliest books, *Ontogeny and Phylogeny*.[28] In this work he covers the background of the recapitulation theory, Haeckel and others, as well as the modern understanding of embryology that shows this to be a much-too-simple conclusion. Why is this important? Of course, it is incumbent on science to move forward and leave behind outdated hypotheses. But Gould's book was written to recover much more than that.

While it is not the case that ontogeny recapitulates phylogeny, it is, however, important to understand the evolutionary relationships between animals and plants, especially at the early developmental stages. The burgeoning field of evolutionary development, or *evo-devo*, as it's commonly called, examines this very thing. Rather than imagine that all organisms go through developmental stages that are identical to adult forms of lower organisms, evo-devo looks at these developmental stages for evidence of ancestral relatedness. The discovery of genes found throughout the animal world that control morphology has greatly stimulated this field. Haeckel's famous statement, while no longer considered valid, finds a faint echo in this line of research.

DEEP TIME

Darwin's model of descent with modification requires gradual change that can only take place if our planet has been around for quite a long time. The age of the earth then became a critical piece of information required by the theory.

Before the advent of scientific methodologies for calculation of the earth's age, assumptions were that either the earth (and the universe) had always existed (Aristotle and other Greeks, for instance), or that the earth and the universe were created at a specific time and therefore had a specific age. What this time might be differed from culture to culture. For instance, in Hindu cosmology, the earth is, at this writing, 1,972,949,108 years old and will exist for a total of 4.32 billion years. In the West, until the eighteenth century, the age of the earth was taken to be defined by the description of creation found in Genesis. Using this as a literal account, writers such as Bishop James Ussher of Ireland calculated that the earth was about six thousand years old. Ussher is famous for concluding that creation began on October 23, 4004 B.C.

Early scientific attempts at age calculations were done with the assumption that the objects in the solar system, including the sun and the earth, began as hot, molten balls that subsequently began cooling. Using this thermodynamic approach, the Scottish physicist Lord Kelvin proposed that the earth was about one hundred million years old. He did not know several key things about the planet, including the nature of its molten core and the effect of radioactive elements. Nonetheless, calculations such as this broke with the Genesis tradition.

Charles Lyell, Darwin's friend and promoter, was an advocate for an age that was much greater than the biblical story supposed. More important, he agreed with the eighteenth-century geologist James Hutton that the features of the planet were best explained by a process of continual change due to geological events such as erosion and volcanism. He defended a *uniformitarian* position with respect to the earth's history, in contrast to the *catastrophism* position that viewed it as in a static state, with occasional changes due to catastrophic events, such as the Noahic flood. Lyell's viewpoint, in agreement as it was with observations being made in the nineteenth century, ultimately became the accepted basis for geological interpretation.

The discovery of radioactivity by Becquerel changed everything. This not only altered the calculations but also provided a basis for determining the age of rocks and, by implication, the age of the planet. Radioactive decay is associated with the release of energy as heat. As a result, the presence of radioactive elements in the makeup of the planet makes calculations of age based on a model of gradual cooling impossible. In addition, because radioactive elements decay at a specific and known rate, defined by quantum mechanical principles, the amount of a particular element in a rock can be used to estimate the age of that rock.

Using radiometric methods, the current value for the age of the earth is 4.54 billion years. Within this time framework it has been determined that life on this planet, at least cellular forms of life, began between 2.7 and 4.4 billion years ago, depending upon the kind of data being analyzed. Of course, Darwin's model does not address the origin of life, but only the origin of species. Nevertheless, critics of evolution continue to refer to it with regard to the beginning of life on the planet. In addition, the more ardent critics, especially those who prefer a literal interpretation of the Judeo-Christian scriptures, or those whose interpretation of science is influenced by these same writings, want to object to the age calculations. These so-called YECs, identified in chapter 3, insist that the planet is, at most, ten thousand years old. Further, they challenge the use of radiometric techniques by arguing that the rate of decay has changed drastically over time, yielding an erroneous age. Of course, geoscientists have refuted these criticisms in detail. Rather than cover them here, we refer you to a website with all of the arguments on both sides clearly spelled out.[29]

BIOLOGICAL SCIENCE THEN, NOW, AND IN THE FUTURE

As a biologist, or, to use the term he would have used to describe himself, as a naturalist, Darwin worked at a time when his discipline was in its infancy. By way of contrast, physics and the related disciplines were mature sciences. What does this mean? One way of thinking about a science as mature is that it has both a theoretical basis and a language in which to discuss the theory. Implicit in this statement are a set of philosophical assumptions about the nature of reality and the task of the science in question in describing that reality.

Physics of the nineteenth century was dominated by the Newtonian paradigm. This included a theoretical framework—the laws of motion and matter as first described so elegantly by Newton—and a language—mathematics. Biology, on the other hand, was still a descriptive activity to which some order had been brought by the classification system of Linnaeus. At the beginning of the nineteenth century, the life sciences had no theoretical foundation and certainly no common language.

Charles Darwin and Gregor Mendel would provide the theoretical foundation from which the language would evolve. By the middle of the twentieth century biology had matured such that it had a theory—the neo-Darwinian fusion of evolution and genetics—and a language—the language of As, Gs, Cs, and Ts that comprise the informational content of the gene. Notice, however, that both theoretical achievements were products of the science of the nineteenth century and, as a result, were imbedded in philosophical assumptions about the scientific enterprise of that time. Thus, both genetics and evolution took their key from the Newtonian worldview that was both reductionistic and deterministic.

The physics of the twentieth and now twenty-first centuries is very different, having undergone a profound *paradigm shift*. This term, much misused in current parlance, was coined by Thomas Kuhn to describe what happens when a science is confronted by anomalous observations.[30] Kuhn suggested that normal science operates with a set of agreed-upon paradigms that dictate the course and interpretation of the research. During the progress of the work, however, observations are made that do not fit these paradigms and are termed anomalies. When such observations continue to be gathered, they may ultimately demand an explanatory model. When this happens, the old paradigm must be modified or completely replaced. Such revolutions are, Kuhn argued, the way that science progresses.

Physics went through such a shift at the beginning of the twentieth century. The quantum revolution changed the way that physics understood the nature of reality. Newtonian mechanics became a special case of a more general view. The clockwork universe with its determinism was replaced by a probabalistic and relativistic picture. Most important, the fundamental interrelatedness of objects and events set the stage for a new model of reality. The resulting change in the philosophy of science applies not only to physics but also to all observational disciplines, including biology.

Until recently, this new direction had no apparent effect on biological research. In fact, the neo-Darwinian synthesis and the molecular approach to genetics so dominated the second half of the twentieth century that most of the life sciences were driven by these paradigms. While lip service was paid to physics, the assumptions of the "new biology" were very much in tune with the nineteenth-century roots of both evolution and genetics. For instance, while the nature of mutational events was understood to be at the atomic and subatomic level, and therefore best described in quantum mechanical terms, the outcome of these events was seen very much in the deterministic Newtonian terms that Darwin him-self would have used. As a result, biological sciences tended to use reduc-tionism not only as a methodology but also as a philosophical position. All of this changed as a consequence of the Human Genome Project.

We have already described the history of this ambitious project taken on by the life science community. The defining moment came paradoxi-cally at the peak of project success, when the sequence had been announced and as the analysis of the massive data set that the genome project generated began. Expectations for the outcome were high. In addition to the perceived medical benefits of knowing the entire genome sequence, the reductionism implicit in the approach would be justified. Everything there is to know about what it means to be human would be located in these critical base sequences.

As we said earlier, the preproject number of human genes was esti-mated to be about one hundred thousand. The first shock came when it was realized that the total was more like twenty to twenty-five thou-sand.[31] Not only is this significantly less than the estimate, it's also not that different from the number of genes present in the fruit fly or the roundworm. The second shock accompanied news of the sequence. The data analysis revealed that the very definition of "gene" must be called into question. It turns out that how one defines a gene alters the count in the database. As Snyder and Gerstein conclude: "Ultimately, we believe that identification of genes based solely on the human genome sequence, while possible in principle, will not be practical in the foreseeable future."[32]

Humans have a number of genes comparable to a worm and we can't even say by looking at the sequence what a gene is. Bad news for reduc-tionism but, it turns out, great news for biology. Molecular biology and the domination it held over the life sciences had run into a brick wall of anomaly. In true Kuhnian fashion, this calls for a paradigm shift. But to what model?

A better picture or model of living systems is one that returns to a view that the whole is greater than the sum of the parts. The cover of *Science* on September 28, 2003, announced the advent of "Networks in Biology." That issue featured a series of papers on applications of network science to biological systems from the molecular to the ecosystem level. Such networks have an interesting feature. They are scale free or small world, as described for a variety of interacting systems. Such networks have the property that they are more than the simple sum of the components.[33] It turns out that the protein products that are encoded by our genes form just such a network in the cell. Therefore, to understand the cell, or a collection of cells that make up an organism, or a collection of organisms, one needs to understand these kinds of networks.

This has precipitated a methodological shift and, more important, a philosophical shift. In terms of tools, genomic scientists now have at their disposal techniques that allow the study of protein interactions. As a result, we see the development of what are now called *interactomes*. These complex network maps describe the array of interactions that can take place within a cell.[34] Beyond this, however, is a change in perspective that has yet to be appreciated. The analysis of data by these tools is no longer reductionistic. The whole can only be understood as having emergent properties, a phrase that for a previous generation of molecular biologists was relegated to the realm of *epiphenomena*, things with no reality, but with only apparent existence. We are in the midst of what may ultimately be seen as a paradigm shift for the life sciences. It will be a few more years before we can say that this has been the case.

DESIGN IN BIOLOGY: WHAT DARWIN COULD AND COULD NOT SEE

*"When I use a word," Humpty Dumpty said in rather a scornful tone, "it
means just what I choose it to mean—neither more nor less."*
*"The question is," said Alice, "whether you CAN make words mean so
many different things."*
"The question is," said Humpty Dumpty, "which is to be master—that's all."
Through the Looking Glass (And What Alice Found There),
Lewis Carroll

One of us, Marty, led off a review of Michael Ruse's wonderful
book, *Darwin and Design*, with this Lewis Carroll quote.[1] Indeed,
the situation remains the same with the word *design* being
bandied about and used to defend this or that position with regard to evolution. And yet, it is the obvious complexity, or even what we might call
design, in nature that attracts our attention, and our scientific wonder.

When Darwin sailed away on the *Beagle*, he was already curious about
the natural world. In fact, it had been this curiosity that pulled him from
a career as either a doctor or a clergyman into the world of science. As
Michael Ruse points out, it is the very complexity of nature, and the
apparent design that we see, which begs for explanation. Complexity and
design attracted Darwin's scientific attention.

The word *design* appears only once in *Origin*, and then in a context that
is critical of those naturalists who are locked into a belief in the unchanging nature of species. In his last chapter ("Recapitulation and
Conclusion"), Darwin refers to the "plan of creation" and the "unity of
design" in reference to this position.[2]

What Darwin does repeat throughout the work, however, is an awareness of the incredible complexity of the living world. He is moved by these observations to say:

> Slow though the process of selection may be, if feeble man can do much by artificial selection, I can see no limit to the amount of change, to the beauty and complexity of the coadaptations between all organic beings, one with another and with their physical conditions of life, which may have been effected in the long course of time through nature's power of selection, that is by the survival of the fittest.[3]

Darwin even concludes his work with his famous "tangled bank" soliloquy, which we reported on in a previous chapter. Darwin is thrilled by the complexity he witnesses in nature, and he cannot refrain from describing it in terms of grandeur:

> There is grandeur in this view of life, with its several powers, having been originally breathed by the Creator into a few forms or into one; and that, whilst this planet has gone circling on according to the fixed law of gravity, from so simple a beginning endless forms most beautiful and most wonderful have been, and are being evolved.[4]

While the word *design* is found only once in *Origin of Species*, it does occur voluminously in Darwin's correspondence. This is especially true of a decades-long exchange he carried out with a colleague who became a close friend, the Harvard University naturalist Asa Gray.

The most prevalent model of the world before Darwin's work was, in fact, that everything, especially every living thing, was the immediate work of the Creator, an Intelligent Designer. *Origin* was a challenge to that idea, presenting a model that depended solely upon a set of naturalistic explanations. Ironically, the modern Intelligent Design theorists find themselves in exactly the same position that Darwin did. They propose a model that attempts to challenge the prevailing paradigm, now Darwin's paradigm. In fact, in many ways they are really only defending an updated version of the earlier nineteenth-century argument already confronted by Darwin himself.

It was the Reverend William Paley, a British cleric, who had, in 1802, put forth what was at that point the most cogent description of what is called *natural theology*. In his book, *Natural Theology, Or Evidences of the Existence and Attributes of the Deity*,[5] Paley argues that the evident design of the natural world, especially with respect to the living world, gives direct proof for the existence of God. His famous watchmaker analogy summarized his arguments and, in our time, gave Richard Dawkins the ammunition for his retort.[6]

THOMAS AQUINAS AND THE FIFTH WAY

Critics call Paley's position the "argument from design," but then go on to erroneously conflate this with St. Thomas Aquinas's "five ways" found in his *Summa Theologia*. Let us pause to remind ourselves of what Thomas actually said.

Thomas's position is distinctly different from Paley's and today's intelligent design movement. Rather than citing evidence of the natural world as proof of God's existence, Thomas begins with the statement that we can, in principle, have no knowledge of God from intellect alone. Instead, he says, we can make analogous statements about God, using as the source for these analogies observations in the natural world. He admits at the beginning that these are only analogies that express in some way what God must be like, but they are not proofs, in Paley's sense. For instance, our common experience is that when something is seen to happen in the natural world, we expect to find a cause for that event. Using Aristotelian logic, Thomas argues that God can be thought of as a first, or primary, cause, a so-called "uncaused cause." He does not mean, however, that God is a cause in the world—only that God can be thought of as *like* a cause.

The design issue is mistakenly tied to the fifth of these analogous ways of knowing which is, in fact, an argument from governance, not design:

> The fifth way is taken from the governance of the world. We see that things which lack intelligence, such as natural bodies, act for an end, and this is evident from their acting always, or nearly always, in the same way, so as to obtain the best result. Hence it is plain that not fortuitously, but designedly, do they achieve their end. Now whatever lacks intelligence cannot move towards an end, unless it be directed by some being endowed with knowledge and intelligence; as the arrow is shot to its mark by the archer. Therefore some intelligent being exists by whom all natural things are directed to their end; and this being we call God.[7]

Here, in the fifth way, Thomas argues from the analogy of an archer shooting an arrow at a target. He says that just as the arrow appears to be directed to some goal, so do things in the world appear to be directed to some end. This uses the Aristotelian concept of *teleology* or purpose. Just as the arrow is directed to the target by the archer, Thomas says, so too things in the world seem to be directed toward some goal (purpose) by some governance, and this is what God must be like—the governance of the world.

PRIMARY AND SECONDARY CAUSES

It is important here to see that Thomas thinks of God as the primary cause of everything. However, just as an arrow moves through the air and is subject to all the laws of physics, in the same way everything in the world is happening according to the same sets of natural laws. Thomas would call all of these events *secondary causes*. It is this part of the natural world that is the province of science.

Darwin, Gray, and their colleagues understood these philosophical distinctions quite clearly, having been gifted with a truly liberal education. In fact, much of their discourse about design relative to Darwin's theory rests on whether primary cause can be invoked to underlie the natural laws, or, as Hume had argued a century before, if primary cause should be ignored altogether. It is unfortunate that the modern commentators on this topic, both those in favor of and those opposed to intelligent design, do not seem to understand the Thomistic distinctions well enough to argue about them.[8]

Asa Gray's position, as expressed in numerous letters exchanged with his good friend Charles Darwin, was that the evolutionary model was not in conflict with his avowed Christian beliefs. In fact, he argued, evolution merely described the set of secondary causes or natural laws that were in operation and that resulted in the observed species diversity of life. In his view, this was merely the working out of the primary cause that was God's act of creation. His arguments are stunningly similar to the position we have called theistic evolution, the most common reaction among scientists and theologians to the challenge of evolution for religious belief.[9]

DARWIN'S OWN EQUIVOCAL RELIGION

Darwin, for his part, was not convinced, although he expressed doubts about the entire issue. Stories of Darwin being an atheist, an agnostic, a faithful Christian, or having a deathbed conversion abound. The real story is much more complex, however, reflecting the way in which his science and his personal life intertwined.

Where Gray was clear about his religious and scientific positions, Darwin was equivocal. He was convinced that his model was correct and all but eliminated any special acts of God in the origin of species. At the same time, the complexity and beauty of the natural world cried out for some kind of purpose. He saw the waste and suffering inherent in the survival of the fittest implicit in natural selection. At the same time, he wanted nature to be moving in a direction that rises above the "red in tooth and claw" world of Tennyson's verse. He was conflicted. As an example of his position, the oft-quoted line regarding the moth and the wasp is used to express his dissatisfaction with the idea of a benevolent Creator. Yet, the entire passage from that letter to Asa Gray partially cited earlier reveals a much more nuanced situation:

> With respect to the theological view of the question; this is always painful to me.—I am bewildered.—I had no intention to write atheistically. But I own that I cannot see, as plainly as others do, & as I should wish to do, evidence of design & beneficence on all sides of us. There seems to me too much misery in the world. I cannot persuade myself that a beneficent & omnipotent God would have designedly created the *Ichneumonidæ* with the express intention of their feeding within the living bodies of caterpillars, or that a cat should play with mice. Not believing this, I see no necessity in the belief that the eye was expressly designed. On the other hand I cannot anyhow be contented to view this wonderful universe & especially the nature of man, & to conclude that everything is the result of brute force. I am inclined to look at everything as resulting from designed laws, with the details, whether good or bad, left to the working out of what we may call chance. Not that this notion *at all* satisfies me. I feel most deeply that the whole subject is too profound for the human intellect. A dog might as well speculate on the mind of Newton.—Let each man hope & believe what he can.[10]

In the end, perhaps it is best to agree with biographers who argue that Darwin became an agnostic toward the end of his life. He was not an aggressive agnostic in the sense that Thomas Huxley was; and he certainly would not embrace the vitrioloic atheism of our contemporary Darwinian, Richard Dawkins. Darwin kept his membership in the Church of England until his death; and in his declining years continued to contribute to the mission society.

We must recognize how Darwin, by his own admission, was confused and, therefore, could not develop a firm theological position. The theodicy problem seemed to overwhelm him. As we have seen, he wondered in his letters to Asa Gray and others how a benevolent Deity could have ordered a world in which extinction was a part of the natural process. At the same time, he marveled at the incredible beauty of creation, almost to the point of religious fervor. He vacillated between belief and unbelief through most of his writings and until the end of his life.

DARWIN ON DESIGN

Darwin was convinced, however, that the living world has a certain design, or, in the more popular modern phrase, a design-like element to it. Michael Ruse makes the point that it was this very evident feature that stoked his curiosity. Was Paley's conclusion correct or, using the tools of science, could Darwin come up with a naturalistic explanation for the occurrence of this design? Descent with modification driven by natural selection is just that—a model that uses only the law-like properties of the observed world. As we have argued above, this model is the best current explanation, the one that has been and continues to be most fruitful.

What then to make of the intelligent design proponents such as Michael Behe and William Dembski? Both of them are scientists: Behe is a biochemist, while Dembski is a mathematician. Neither of them can be called creationists, if by that we mean either biblical literalists or scientific creationists. They both accept deep time. They both see the evolutionary model as the explanation for much of the variation observed in the living world. It's just that they want to rescue some of Paley's natural theology. They insist on holding out for the influence of an intelligent designer at certain key points in the process. They argue that Darwin's explanation is incomplete and cannot account for instances of "irreducible" or "specified" complexity.[11] They argue that gradual mutational change cannot be called upon to result in such features as the bacterial flagellum or the human eye. Thus, these must have been the product of an intelligent designer.

We have already discussed the religious reactions to Darwin's theory in our chapter on the many theologies of evolution (chapter 3). It is certainly true that the ID movement has as a subtext a similar theological objection, especially to the atheistic materialism that tends to overlay the evolutionary argument of certain scientific fundamentalists. It is also the case, as we have seen, that the attempts to insert ID into the public school curriculum in the United States have been legally banned because of this religious agenda. We will not discuss these issues further here. Instead, we would like to consider the scientific and philosophical arguments that are made for ID versus the naturalistic explanation of the Darwinian model.

DARWIN VERSUS DESIGN

To begin with, there is a scientific, or perhaps methodological, question that needs to be addressed. The objection raised by ID against the neo-Darwinian model is that strict gradualism, the step-by-step mutational set of events that change the genetic information one base pair at a time, cannot explain the development of these complex systems. How could selection work for a feature that is only the end result of the process, and not evident in the gradually altered intermediates? The problem is that the standard Darwinian model assumes strict gradualism as the only mechanism for evolutionary change. True, this is the position of some of the hardliners such as Richard Dawkins.

However, the array of available mechanisms in modern evolutionary biology is much richer than that, and includes everything from single base changes to symbiotic acquisitions.[12] Indeed, the very cells that make up our marvelous bodies are themselves the products of such events. Lynn Margulis has proposed the endosymbiotic model for the occurrence of the cells of eukaryotic organisms. She argues that at some point in our biological history, two cells merged, one engulfing the other, to result in a living form with greater evolutionary potential. In the case of animals, this yielded cells containing nuclei, the home of our genetic information, and mitochondria, energy factories of our cells. This event was not a gradual one and, in fact, resulted in what some call the "eukaryotic big bang," with a sudden (in geological terms) radiation of these new forms of life.

Therefore, in methodological terms ID argues against only one mechanism of the evolutionary model. Yes, it is true that Darwin did not know about genes or about endosymbiosis. Yes, it is also true that evolutionary biologists continue to debate the relative contributions of these various mechanisms. However, it is not correct to build an entire counterargument based on the faulty assumption of only one possible mechanism.

There are also a couple of philosophical flaws in the ID proposal. First, in the case of Michael Behe's understanding of irreducible complexity, he makes the following argument: since irreducible complexity examples can be described that cannot be accounted for with data that rely upon naturalistic explanations, such structures must have been intelligently designed. The difficulty here is classically called an "argument from ignorance." When such arguments are used in theological frameworks, they are referred to as "God of the gaps" explanations. It goes something like this: we can't discern a naturalistic way to get from A to F, so therefore God must have intervened to cover the gap. The logical difficulty with this is that, as soon as the naturalistic explanations are found that yield the sequence A-B-C-D-E-F, then the need for the God explanation disappears. This has turned out to be the case for each of the irreducibly complex examples in Behe's book, as specific examples are shown that have perfectly good Darwinian mechanisms without the need to invoke intervention.

The second philosophical flaw with the ID proposal concerns the concept of causation. Darwin and Gray argued about this from an understanding of the arguments of Aquinas as well as the counterproposal of Hume. However, it is not at all the case that the modern ID theorists and their opponents are aware of the issues in this instance. To this flaw we now turn.

William Dembski holds that there are two kinds of causes: natural causes and intelligent causes. What are these? Both Thomas Aquinas and David Hume would understand natural causes to be secondary causes and certainly the targets for explanation by observational science. But what do we make of "intelligent causes?" Are these another class of secondary cause? If so, then they are completely subject to the scientific method, as are all such causes in the natural world. Or does he mean that such causes are specific to the action of the Intelligent Designer . . . in this case, God? If so, then does he mean to say "primary cause" here? Again, both Aquinas and Hume would have understood that primary cause was an analogous statement about God's action, and not actually a cause in the world as other efficient causes are. While Aquinas used this analogy to say something about God, Hume rejected it as having nothing to do with the way science should be carried out.

It appears, however, that the ID proponents want to have it both ways, which it cannot, by definition, be. They wish to have intelligent causes be considered as part of the observable and measurable and, at the same time, ascribe them directly to the Designer as interventions in the natural process. This logical flaw of confusing primary with secondary causation does not seem to deter the ID community in its quest for scientific acceptance.

If ID is a scientifically and philosophically flawed theory, does that mean that the only alternative is the evolutionary biology coupled with fundamentalist atheism that is the hallmark of Richard Dawkins? While it is not time to throw out the scientific enterprise in favor of a return to Aristotle, it is the case that, as it is supposed to do, science is changing.

Evolutionary biology is not static. New evidence arises that demands revisions of this most dynamic model. The late Stephen Jay Gould was keenly aware of some of these issues in his field. In order to account for what he perceived to be difficulties, he explored new avenues, including such concepts as punctuated equilibrium and exaptation.[13] More recently, the evidence from comparative genomics, systems biology, and the importance of horizontal gene transfer are changing the theoretical landscape of biology. As we have mentioned, Goldenfeld and Woese have suggested that the very concept of species, the central topic of Darwin's book, may be in need of re-definition.[14]

It turns out that Darwin's "tangled bank" picture of the living world may, in fact, be the most apt current description. Living things exist as a complex web of interactions, from the proteins within the cells to the organisms within the ecosphere. Within this web is a constant exchange of information, both horizontally and vertically. In fact, the flow of biological information may overcome even the definitive barriers that were so evident to Charles Darwin, upsetting his scientific sensibilities but, in the end, leaving his theory intact.

WHAT DOES IT MEAN TO BE HUMAN?

J ust what does Darwin's theory of evolution do to human dignity? If Darwin could write about the predecessor of our human race as "a hairy quadruped, furnished with a tail and pointed ears, probably arboreal in habits," does this detract from our self-understanding as spiritual beings? If we human beings are nothing more than the result of our biological evolution, are we reduced in some way? Are we less than we might have thought ourselves to be? Does our status fall as we realize we are animals, and only animals? Sir Julian Huxley certainly interpreted Darwin this way. In his introduction to a modern edition of the sixth edition of *Origin*, he wrote: "Man could no longer be regarded as the Lord of Creation, a being apart from the rest of nature."[1]

It has become common wisdom that with each new scientific development, the human person gets knocked down a peg, or knocked out of the center of importance. In his Introductory *Lectures on Psycho-Analysis*, Sigmund Freud said that the human race has been knocked off its high horse three times. The first was the Copernican revolution that removed the earth from the center of the universe in favor of heliocentrism. Allegedly this rearrangement of the sun and planet also removed humankind from the center of the universe and gave it only marginal value. Second, many with Freud like to say the Darwinian revolution reduced humankind to the rank of an animal, demoting us from our previous rank as God's special creature. Third, Freud showed the ego is not the master of its own house.[2] Allegedly, these three revolutions have taken away our human dignity by marginalizing us and animalizing us. There may be coming a fourth. Some forecast still another shock in store for the human race on that future day when we make contact with extraterrestrial intelligent life (ETIL). When that day comes, it is frequently said, our previous self-delusion that we are the only intelligent beings in this vast universe will be overcome by reality shock. After being knocked off our high horse three times or maybe even four times, we might get the message that we should feel more humble than we have in the past. So goes popular cultural logic. In what follows, we will look at this logic more carefully.

First, there is no evidence in theological literature or religious consciousness that the Copernican revolution in science led to a decentering of humanity in culture or faith. The Copernican revolution was a scientific revolution, to be sure; but the widespread belief that human consciousness felt demoted by it lacks any historical credibility. In fact, one objection to the heliocentric viewpoint was that it elevated the earth and mankind above our acceptable station. Since Greek times, our planet had been thought to consist of fire, air, water, and earth. The other planets were part of the fifth element, the *quintessence*. With the earth placed among these exalted planets, we were given a status we did not deserve.[3] If anything, the subsequent rise of humanism during the eighteenth century Enlightenment demonstrates no loss of a sense of center on the part of human consciousness.

Second, when it comes to the Darwinian revolution, the impact has been ambiguous. On the one hand, we now understand the human race to be one member of a larger class of primates. We are animals through and through. Perhaps one might interpret this as a demotion, as a drop in rank from our previous self-understanding. On the other hand, Darwinism provides a scale for measuring lower and higher animals; and we human beings find ourselves on the top of that animal scale. What makes humankind higher than our animal relatives is that we are more highly evolved, more intelligent, and we have a more developed moral sense. So, what seems to have been taken away by our demotion to animality is given back by our promotion on a scale of evolutionary value. Our dignity has been rescued by the incipient doctrine of progress laid on top of the history of our biology.

Third, by burying the powerful forces of our id in an unconscious over which the superego has to fight to gain control, our ego—our conscious self—seems to lose its independence. We become victims of the battle between primordial urges and habits ingrained in us by our mothers during toilet training. Like a slave struggling for freedom, our egos struggle to overcome an internal determinism. This picture of human nature might suggest that the human person, identified with the ego, has been swallowed up by forces beyond its control. However, a closer look will show that we have not given in to those forces. The very development of the field of professional psychotherapy along with the proliferation of psychotechnologies offered in self-help books demonstrates an indefatigable desire on the part of the human race to gain control. No determinism, either external or internal, will marginalize the ambitious human spirit. Freud may not have overestimated his influence on the Western mind; but he did miss the target on this matter.

Fourth, is it really accurate to forecast a demotion in human importance should we make contact with ETIL? We will take a look at this question in some detail. What is decisive is the set of assumptions we make when imagining what beings living on other worlds might be like.

Curiously, the assumptions made by serious scientists regarding life on other worlds are an export from earth of the evolutionary story as they have constructed it. What has happened on earth is likely to be duplicated elsewhere. And if evolution has been going on longer on another planet, then we can expect to meet intelligent beings that are more highly evolved than we. This is the key assumption made by astro-biologists and other stargazers involved in the Search for Extraterrestrial Intelligence (SETI). What we expect to show in the next paragraphs is that this projection onto the heavens of earth's evolution exhibits sublimated religious sensibilities. Even more: it seeks the equivalent of scientific salvation from the stars. The result is a surreptitious re-endorsement of the importance of human life on the earth. In short, none of the four apparent challenges to our centrality will prevent humankind from remounting its high horse.

What is at stake theologically for Christian anthropology are two things: understanding the human race as embodying the image of God (the *imago Dei*) and thereby possessing dignity; plus understanding the human race as alienated from God by sin, by subjection to evil, suffering, and death. Just how taking Darwinian evolution into theological anthropology ought to be done is a matter of continued religious concern.

LOWER AND HIGHER RACES

When the topic is human dignity, the ideology of progress stands up and says, "look at me." Yes, as we have tried to show, Darwin himself was ambiguous regarding the role of progress; and today's laboratory scientists reject progress in basic biology. Yet, it is next to impossible to disentangle evolutionary biology from the cultural belief in progress. Biology comes to us shrink-wrapped in ideology. When the topic is human dignity, it is to the realm of the intersection of science and culture that we must turn.

In the nineteenth-century view, species are ranked. Some are higher. Others are lower. The more complex and developed species are higher. The best are the most highly evolved. Built into this ranking is the doctrine of progress, according to which evolving changes over time lead progressively to improvements.

According to Darwin, the species we observe today have been victorious in the struggle for life. They are the most fit. And the most fit are ranked highest on the evolutionary scale.

> The inhabitants of the world at each successive period in its history have beaten their predecessors in the race for life, and are, in so far, higher in the scale, and their structure has generally become more specialized; and this may account for the common belief held by so many paleontologists, that organization on the whole has progressed . . . old forms having been supplanted by new and improved forms of life, the products of Variation and the Survival of the Fittest.[4]

When Darwin applies his theory of inherited variation and natural selection to the human phenomenon, the same principles obtain. Because of the principle of descent with modification, Darwin sought to emphasize the continuity between humanity and its predecessors in the animal kingdom. No radical break between us and our ancestors can, in principle, be located. Whether we like it or not, we are animals, even if very intelligent animals. "The difference in mind between man and the higher animals, great as it is, is certainly one of degree and not of kind."[5]

After debating with himself whether the human race evolved from a single origin (monogenesis) or multiple origins (polygenesis), he concludes that all the races we currently see derived from a single set of successive developments. We human beings descended from a common ancestor we share with higher primates such as orangutans and chimpanzees. As the human race spread out geographically, over time the various human races developed independently. Should we now consider the various races as separate species? As separate subspecies? Darwin notes that when persons of two races marry and have children, the crossing of the races yields children with inherited traits from both parents. This would suggest that all races belong to the same species. Yet, Darwin finds he is unsure whether each race constitutes a species or subspecies. He tentatively describes them as subspecies.

On the one hand, Darwin is struck with the significant differences between the races in skin color, bone structure, and what he sees as mental capacities. Darwin satisfies himself to believe that the civilized European races are much more intelligent than the aborigines who live in Africa, America, and Australia. The latter he calls "savages," to distinguish them from the more highly developed Europeans. On the other hand, Darwin admits puzzlement. Aboard the Beagle, he spent time with such savages. He was amazed that they could think like he does.

> Yet, I was incessantly struck, whilst living with the Fuegians on board the Beagle, with the many little traits of character, shewing how similar their minds were to ours; and so it was with a full-blooded negro with whom I happened once to be intimate.[6]

Despite this acknowledged parity of mental ability, Darwin remains ambivalent. At the level of assumption, Darwin ranked the various races as lower and higher, with his own race sitting on top of the ranking.

LOWER AND HIGHER MORALITY

Our moral sense evolves. As members of a species develop socially and find they must depend upon one another for survival, opines Darwin, the fittest find they belong to more fully integrated societies. Contemporary sociobiologists refer to this social behavior as *altruism*, meaning that at times the best interests of an individual might be sacrificed on behalf of the larger group's adaptive success. Darwin uses terms such as "sympathy" and "love" to analyze cooperative behavior that would lead to survival for the fittest groups. When one enters the domain of sympathy and love, then the question of a moral sense arises.

The moral sense—the ability to distinguish right from wrong and exhibit regret for past wrongs and anticipate better from worse plans for the future—has evolved in humanity in stages. The earliest stage would consist of sympathy and service toward other members of one's own family or tribe, what today many call *kin altruism*. Over time this would expand to include additional groups beyond one's own tribe, what today many call *reciprocal altruism*. Finally, when we arrive at the stage of liberal Western society, a doctrine of universal humanity would develop; and we would find we can show love to all human beings, whether close kin or distant strangers. This is the highest form of moral sense, the most evolved.

Darwin tells the story of moral evolution chronologically:

> Finally, the social instincts which no doubt were acquired by man, as by the lower animals, for the good of the community, will from the first have given to him some wish to aid his fellows, and some feeling of sympathy. Such impulses will have served him at a very early period as a rude rule of right and wrong. But as man gradually advanced in intellectual power and was enabled to trace the more remote consequences of his action; as he acquired sufficient knowledge to reject baneful customs and superstitions; as he regarded more and more not only the welfare but the happiness of his fellow-men; as from habit, following on beneficial experience, instruction, and example, his sympathies became more tender and widely diffused, so as to extend to the men of all races, to the imbecile, the maimed, and other useless members of society, and finally to the lower animals,—so would the standard of his morality rise higher and higher.[7]

On Darwin's scale of morality, love for all members of the human race as well as love for all creatures ranks higher than either brute selfishness or even tribal loyalty. What leads to higher morality is increased intelligence gained over a lengthy evolutionary history of advance.

Darwin's theory of biological evolution converged with Herbert Spencer's belief in human evolution. As we have already pointed out, this convergence became known as social Darwinism, an ethic to guide social, political, and economic relations. The key assumption in social Darwinism is this: "The conduct to which we apply the name good, is the relatively more evolved conduct; and that bad is the name we apply to conduct which is relatively less evolved."[8]

FROM LOWER RELIGION
TO HIGHER SCIENCE

The religious sense evolves. It begins with primitive superstition. It progresses upward toward monotheism. Then, finally, religion arrives at the level of its own supersession, science. So thinks Darwin.

At the most primitive level, the level of the savage, "belief in unseen or spiritual agencies . . . seems almost universal with the less civilized races." Darwin compares savages with dogs. He compares "the tendency in savages to imagine that natural objects and agencies are animated by spiritual or living essences" to a dog's reaction to a parasol being blown by an invisible breeze; the dog would bark at the invisible wind as if it were a living creature.[9] Archaic peoples attributed living traits to unseen and mysterious forces. This gave rise to belief in the world of spirits. Superstitious beliefs make uncivilized people higher than the animals; but they remain lower than what would come later.

Gradually, belief in the world of the spirits gave way to higher forms of belief, belief in multiple gods and then later belief in a single god. Such a belief projects onto the unseen screen the drama of human affection and passion. "The belief in spiritual agencies would easily pass into belief in the existence of one or more gods. For savages would naturally attribute to spirits the same passions, the same love of vengeance or simplest form of justice, and the same affections which they themselves experienced."[10] The resultant feeling of devotion to the divine includes a sense of dependence, reverence, fear, gratitude, and hope for the future. The mental complexity appropriate to this set of beliefs is evidence of advanced development. Only those ranked higher on the evolutionary scale are capable of such religious belief. "No being could experience so complex an emotion until advanced in his intellectual and moral faculties to at least a moderately high level."[11]

This level of advanced religious belief does not end the evolutionary story, however. The human race can rise still higher. We are capable of rising above the superstitions of religion to the level of science. With science, we are able to review the history of religion with moral condemnation and intellectual disdain:

> The same high mental faculties which first led man to believe in unseen spiritual agencies, then in fetishism, polytheism, and ultimately in monotheism, would infallibly lead him, as long as his reasoning powers remained poorly developed, to various strange superstitions and customs. Many of these are terrible to think of—such as the sacrifice of human beings to a blood-loving god; the trial of innocent persons by the ordeal of poison or fire; witchcraft, &c.—yet it is well occasionally to reflect on these superstitions, for they shew us what an infinite debt of gratitude we owe to the improvement of our reason, to science, and our accumulated knowledge.[12]

In sum, although complex religious belief systems indicate a level of mental reasoning superior to the animals from whom we have evolved, human beings are capable of further development in intellectual capabilities that lead to a surpassing of religion and entering the domain of scientific reasoning and knowledge. At the top of the intellectual hierarchy we find those segments of the human race who have transcended religious superstition and entered the halls of science.

This evolutionary hierarchy attempts to describe the phenomenon we know as *religion*. What about the distinctively *theological* question? What about the question: does God exist? Are we actually responsible to a divine reality? A mere description of religion's evolution cannot answer this theological question. Darwin recognizes this, and he honors it. He honors this question without making a personal commitment. The higher question, he says, is "whether there exists a Creator and Ruler of the universe." Then he observes, "this has been answered in the affirmative by the highest intellects that have ever lived."[13] Although Darwin adroitly avoids making a commitment of his own, it should be observed that he attributes an affirmative answer to "the highest intellects that have ever lived." That is, those persons with the greatest reasoning powers believe in God. Those most highly evolved—those minds capable of science—affirm belief in the divine reality. In short, theological affirmations of God stand equal with scientific reasoning in the evolutionary hierarchy.

In sum, it appears that the theory of evolution has in no way compromised our human sense of self-worth, our conferral of dignity upon ourselves. Whether due merely to our stubborn egoism or due to the fact that God confers dignity upon us with the *imago Dei*, all the theory of evolution has done is allow us to shift the locus of dignity from our origin to our future. Our sense of worth is the end result of a long development—perhaps even an ongoing process; it is not something belonging to our origin. In "By an Evolutionist," Alfred Tennyson gives voice to the era.

> If my body come from brutes, tho' somewhat
>   finer than their own,
>   I am heir, and this my kingdom. Shall
>   the royal voice be mute?
> No, but if the rebel subject seek to drag
>   me from the throne,
>   Hold the sceptre, Human Soul, and rule
>   thy province of the brute.
>
> I have climb'd to the snows of Age, and I
>   gaze at a field in the Past,

Where I sank with the body at times in
 the sloughs of a low desire,
But I hear no yelp of the beast, and the
 Man is quiet at last,
As he stands on the heights of his life
 with a glimpse of a height that is higher.

EXTRATERRESTRIAL EVOLUTION?

What arrogance we earthlings have! We think that we are the best! And we think that we are the only intelligent beings in the universe! In the nearly unlimited expanse of outer space, there must be millions, if not billions, of civilizations. When we make contact, this will knock us off our high horse. Right? So goes the rhetoric of the tabloids.

If we turn from the tabloids to serious science, to the field of astrobiology, we find speculation about life in space in three forms. First, we might export life from earth to inhabit another planet, perhaps Mars. Some NASA scientists would like to terraform Mars—that is, plant life on the red planet. Second, we will search for non-intelligent life forms, perhaps microbial life at an early stage in evolution. We call this "exobiology," now a subfield within astrobiology. Exobiologists are looking for extraterrestrial non-intelligent life (ETNL) on Mars and the moons of both Saturn and Jupiter. Third, we will seek to discover the existence of extraterrestrial intelligent life (ETIL), more than likely living on planets outside our solar system yet still within the Milky Way. SETI—the search for extraterrestrial intelligence—is the most sophisticated institution dedicated to this task. SETI's method is to listen for radio signals being transmitted from extraterrestrial civilizations. To date, no such signals have been detected.

Here we might ask: how does Charles Darwin's theory of evolution relate to the question of extraterrestrial intelligent life? First, we need to note how Darwin insists repeatedly that his work describes the origin of species; it does not describe the origin of life itself. This mysterious origin is not explained by the theory of evolution. The theory of evolution "as yet throws no light on the far higher problem of the essence or origin of life."[14] Once life has begun, Darwin can tell us how it led to variations and eventually to new species. Further, the theory is fertile in that it predicts further evolution over time. Not all of Darwin's followers, however, limit the theory of evolution to speciation. They expand it to cover the origin of life. Then they project it onto other worlds.

What the Darwinian model does is provide a theory to describe the history of life on planet Earth. What about other planets? Even though the theory of evolution has nothing to say about the origin of life, we may ask: can it still predict that life would originate independently on other planets and then follow Darwin's path of evolution? Many scientists of our own era believe this is the case. Their application of the Darwinian model includes the assumption that life's origination is included in the theory; and they further contend that what has happened on the earth must have also happened in many locations only dimly seen through our telescopes.

The research enterprise of astrobiology begins with the search for a hospitable home for earthlike life. What is necessary, astrobiogists think, is a planet roughly the size of the earth with similar gravity, metal rich, and sufficiently distant from its respective sun in order to provide liquid water. To support life, such a planet should be like the porridge Goldilocks preferred to eat, not too hot and not too cold. And such a planet would need to remain stable and safe for a long period of time, perhaps years numbered in the billions. To date, there is no empirical evidence that a Goldilocks planet exists. However, the wobble effect of perhaps 200 or more planets orbiting stars have been catalogued. It might be only a matter of time before the Goldilocks home for life is discovered.

That we are likely to find the Goldilocks planet is not a matter of dispute among scientists. What is a matter of dispute is the likelihood of finding evolving life that fits the Darwinian model. Those who believe evolution would be duplicated on an extraterrestrial planet are called *contact optimists*. The doubters affirm the *uniqueness hypothesis*. Doubters believe the evolutionary history of planet Earth is unique; and the probability of its being duplicated elsewhere is so low as to throw a wet blanket over contact optimism.

Evolutionary assumptions are everywhere at work in astrobiology. "Everything evolves," is a cardinal SETI doctrine.[15] The list of astrobiological assumptions is by no means limited to species evolution. This list includes the assumption that life will originate where Goldilocks conditions are present. Life *must* evolve wherever the conditions are right; and there simply *must* be extraterrestrial planets where this is possible. "Life is the product of deterministic forces," writes Nobel Prize–winning biologist Christian de Duve.

> Life was bound to arise under the prevailing conditions, and it will arise similarly wherever and whenever the same conditions obtain. There is

hardly any room for "lucky accidents" in the gradual, multi-step process whereby life originated. This conclusion is compellingly enforced when one considers the development of life as a chemical process.[16]

As long as the right chemical conditions exist somewhere in outer space—in the Goldilocks location—we can expect life to evolve and develop and progress. And, perhaps, some day we will make contact with this extraterrestrial intelligent life form.

After adding the origin of life to the evolutionary model, contact optimists then add Darwin's theory regarding human moral and religious evolution. Key here is the belief in moral progress: the more highly evolved, the higher the moral value. These assumptions fill SETI enthusiasts with excitement. They give apparent justification for contact optimism. Because evolution includes progress, when we find extraterrestrial civilizations that have existed longer and progressed further, they will represent our own future coming back to speed up our evolution. Extraterrestrial intelligent beings will be more advanced than we earthlings in matters of both science and morality; so they will be able to help us advance more quickly. We might even view ETIL as offering earth a form of science-based salvation. An implicit doctrine of terrestrial salvation wrought by more advanced extraterrestrials embellishes the term *optimism* for the contact optimists.

Here is how SETI's Frank Drake gives voice to speculations based on contact optimism.

> Everything we know says there are other civilizations out there to be found. The discovery of such civilizations would enrich our civilization with valuable information about science, technology, and sociology. This information could directly improve our abilities to conserve and to deal with sociological problems—poverty for example. Cheap energy is another potential benefit of discovery, as are advancements in medicine.[17]

Note how this optimism extends well beyond mere contact with extraterrestrial intelligence. It includes optimism regarding the solution to "sociological" problems such as poverty and energy while giving us a leap forward in medicine. It takes the form of secular salvation.

Physicist Paul Davies carries his speculations beyond sociology to spirituality.

> It is clear that if we receive a message from an alien community, it will not have destroyed itself . . . it is overwhelmingly probable that the aliens concerned will be far more advanced than us. . . . we can expect that if we receive a message, it will be from beings who are very advanced indeed in all respects, ranging from technology and social development to an understanding of nature and philosophy.[18]

Davies proceeds to engage in theological speculation based on his assumptions regarding extraterrestrial superiority due to their more advanced stage in evolution. "It is a sobering fact that we would be at a stage of spiritual development very inferior to that of almost all of our intelligent alien neighbors."[19] Davies reflects Darwin's own precedent, namely, human evolution begins with rude superstition, passes through polytheism to monotheism and even to science. And, along with these advances, we find an evolution of a higher moral sense, a love for all races and all creatures. This assumption seems to warrant speculation that extraterrestrial intelligent beings will be more advanced in morality than we earthlings are.

Some SETI scientists look forward to deliverance from earth's religions. After all, religion belongs to our savage past, to the bygone age of superstition. Perhaps ETIL can bring us enlightenment, a postreligious scientific enlightenment. Jill Tarter speculates that the "long-lived extraterrestrials either never had, or have outgrown, organized religion."[20]

Cornell University's Carl Sagan embraced such contact optimism, to be sure; but he registered awareness that such speculation carries the astrobiologist well beyond the limits of what can be empirically known. "I would guess that the Universe is filled with beings far more intelligent, far more advanced than we are. But, of course, I might be wrong. Such a conclusion is at best based on a plausibility argument, derived from the numbers of planets, the ubiquity of organic matter, the immense timescales available for evolution, and so on. It is not a scientific demonstration."[21]

We see here how contact optimists have taken a number of nonempirical and speculative steps, beginning with Darwin's model of evolutionary progress and projecting hopes and dreams onto celestial beings expected to be living around those tiny dots of light we see in our heavens. Extrapolating from our own evolutionary history into the future, we can construct images of ETIL more advanced in intelligence, in science, and even in spirituality. Might these more advanced intelligences represent our own future? And, if they would come to visit us, might they represent our own future coming to rescue us from taking the wrong evolutionary fork? Might an extraterrestrial science come to the earth to supplement our own science and solve the earth's problems? Might science in its extraterrestrial form become the earth's savior? So tempting are the ideological overlays of progress, social Darwinism, and atheistic materialism that the projection of evolution onto other planets takes the astrobiologist well beyond what can be considered empirical science.

UNIQUE-EARTH SCIENTISTS

Not all evolutionary biologists place themselves in the contact optimism camp, however. Those holding the uniqueness hypothesis are critical of contact optimism. When the former president of the American Association for the Advancement of Science, Francisco Ayala, poses the question regarding the possible existence of extraterrestrial intelligence, he says, "My answer is an unequivocal 'no.'" Why? Ayala contends that what has happened in our planet's evolutionary history has been contingent, not guided by an internal purpose or entelechy. Progress is not built into the long history of evolution. Belief in progress is an ideological overlay.

Ayala argues that if we on the earth were to replay "life's tape" from the beginning of life to the present, the course of evolution would not repeat itself. According to existing evolutionary history, for the first two billion years only microbes existed on the earth. The eukaryotes were the first organisms whose cells had a nucleus containing DNA. And, adds Ayala, there is nothing in the process that would make it likely that multicellular organisms would evolve. Evolution could have stopped right there. No animals might have come into existence. "We know that animals evolved only once. So, there is little likelihood that animals would arise again, if life's tape were replayed."

In each chapter of the evolutionary story, we find a long concatenation of contingent, if not unique, events. We find millions of random mutations and environmental circumstances, all points where the history could have taken a different turn. The probability of a repeat of this history is so low as to be virtually nonexistent. The evolutionary process would produce a different outcome every time it gets going. If we "replay life's tape," the improbabilities would get multiplied from year to year, from generation to generation, millions and millions of times.

The resulting improbabilities are of such magnitude that even if there would be millions of universes as large as the universe that we know, the products (improbability of humans x number of suitable planets) would not cancel out by many orders of magnitude. The improbabilities apply not only to *Homo sapiens*, but also to "intelligent organisms with which we could communicate"; by this phrase I mean organisms with a brain-like organ that would allow them to think and to communicate, and with senses somewhat like ours (seeing, hearing, touching, smelling, tasting) which would allow them to get information from the environment and to communicate intelligently with other organisms. We have to conclude that humans are alone in the immense universe and that we forever will be alone.[22]

What we see here is a disagreement between two schools of Darwinian thought, the contact optimists and those who hypothesize that the earth has a unique and unrepeatable evolutionary history. Both are Darwinian. One builds into its speculations the doctrine of progress and the belief that higher stages in evolution have a moral valence. The other denies that progress is built into the process of species development; and it denies that empirical grounds exist for speculating how extraterrestrial intelligent beings would necessarily be our scientific, moral, or religious superiors.

THE IMAGE OF GOD AND HUMAN DIGNITY

As cited above, Julian Huxley seems to think that Darwin's theory of evolution puts an end to the human lordship over creation. Is this really the case? Let's remind ourselves of just what is at stake here. In the opening chapter of the book of Genesis we read:

> Then God said, "Let us make humankind in our image, according to our likeness; and let them have dominion over the fish of the sea, and over the birds of the air, and over the cattle, and over all the wild animals of the earth, and over every creeping thing that creeps upon the earth."
> So God created humankind in his image, in the image of God he created them; male and female he created them. (vv. 26–27)

The use of the term "dominion" connotes lordship, to be sure; so perhaps Huxley may be justified in using this term to describe what the ancient

Hebrews along with contemporary Jews, Muslims, and Christians believe about the relationship of the human race to the rest of creation. Has this special status been lost because of Darwin?

No. The answer is "no" for two reasons. First, on our planet Earth the human race has no competitors for this rank. As of yet, no species of plants or animals has invented a technology akin to cell phones and computers that work, at least some of the time. No beehive has ever established a university. Although certain species of red ants (such as the *Formica polyerges rufescens* and *Formica sanguine*) enslave a species of black ants (*Formica fusca*) and make the black ants do all the work of sustaining the superior tribe,[23] to date no species of ants has enslaved *Homo sapiens*. Furthermore, many leaders in today's human race so acutely feel the responsibility of lordship or dominion that we are organizing to care for our planet, to love our earth, and to work toward its sustainability. No other species bears this moral burden. No one realistically foresees another of earth's species carrying this moral burden, let alone leading an animal insurrection to unseat the human race. Neither theologically nor culturally has Darwinism pulled the throne out from under the human derrière.

The second reason is, as we have seen, that Darwin's model of evolution may include a doctrine of progress with an accompanying scale of value. The human race is judged to be the most progressive. Human lordship is enabled by human intelligence; and human dignity is grounded in the human moral sense. If we were to adopt the Darwinian hierarchy produced by evolutionary advance, no loss to human status would be incurred.

Having said this, we need to point out that Christian theologians do not ground human dignity in the doctrine of progress, let alone in the superiority we humans enjoy over the animal and plant kingdoms. Rather, human dignity is grounded in the image of God, the *imago Dei*. The *imago Dei* is granted to the human race in two phases, an original natural phase, as we see it in the Genesis 1:26-27 text above, as well as a future redemption phase. Because the image of the divine in us seems so difficult to see—it is difficult to see because we are alienated from God by the darkness of sin—the New Testament promises a future restoration or even a fulfillment of the incipient image. Jesus Christ is the image of God (*eikon tou Theou*) into which all members of the human race will be grafted. Jesus' Easter resurrection is "the first fruits" (1 Cor 15:20) of a resurrection into divine perfection that we will all share. Our dignity today is contingent on God's future ratification and fulfillment of that dignity at the advent of the new creation, which includes our resurrection.

What grounds our dignity as human beings is not our centrality in the universe; we are valuable not because other planets orbit around ours. Nor is it that we stand higher than the other animals with whom we share our earth. Our dignity as human beings is not the result of some sort of superiority over possible competitors. Rather, our dignity is a gift to us from God, a gift of sharing in God's own dynamic life. This would be the Christian belief with or without the concept of evolution.

Vatican theologians put it this way:

> Created in the image of God, human beings are by nature bodily and spiritual, men and women made for one another, persons oriented toward communion with God and with one another, wounded by sin and in need of salvation, and destined to be conformed to Christ, the perfect image of the Father, in the power of the Holy Spirit.[24]

Lutheran Joshua Mortiz puts it this way: "Humans are the image of God, not by biological nature or right, but through *election* from among the animals by divine grace. As human *animals* by form and nature, we are biological *priests* by vocation."[25] It is God's call to the human race while within the animal kingdom that imparts the divine image and endows us with dignity.

If anything, the placing of the human race squarely within the animal kingdom provides resources for theologians to understand better the phenomenon of sin. Although we ordinarily identify sin with willful acts of disobedience, in the human condition sin comes in a single package with a destiny characterized by violence, suffering, and death. These are signs of our alienation from our creator God. Recent ethological studies show more and more the continuity between human behavior and animal behavior, especially surprising commonalities between higher primates and *Homo sapiens*. In addition to violence due to the need to kill to eat, gratuitous violence motivated by malevolence can be found in both human and nonhuman activities.

Contemporary evolutionary biologists believe we *Homo sapiens* share a common six-million-year-old ancestor with higher primates—such as chimpanzees, gorillas, bonobos, and orangutans. As in human society, we find among these nonhuman relatives of ours such behaviors as deceit, rape, murder, and even genocide. What we find in these groups of primates, most intensely among chimpanzees, is organized gangs of males who protect territory and expand territory; and they are willing to kill all rivals, sometimes with savage disregard for the feelings of their victims. "Human savagery is not unique. It is shared by other party-gang species. . . . Our ape ancestors have passed to us a legacy, defined by the power of natural selection and written in the molecular chemistry of DNA," write Richard Wrangham and Dale Peterson.[26] Might the Darwinian placing of human beings within the animal realm illustrate what Christian theology has long called the "fallenness" of creation, and the need not just for human redemption but for a "new creation"?

We find ourselves in a situation of ambiguity. On the one hand, we *Homo sapiens* share with all of life the predator-prey relationship in which the prey dies so that the predator might live. We share with all of life what Darwin calls the "struggle for existence" and Spencer calls the "survival of the fittest." In addition, we share with some forms of life gratuitous violence, destructive activity that adds freely elected sin on top of the already unavoidable struggle. Yet, on the other hand, we still maintain that human beings have dignity. "While the *imago Dei* is impaired or disfigured, it cannot be destroyed by sin . . . the ontological structure of the image, while affected in its historicity by sin, remains despite the reality of sinful actions."[27]

Having said all of this, we still need to acknowledge that collapsing human origins into the evolution of animals makes the religious mind a bit nervous. There does exist some fear of ontological reductionism, a fear that we human beings will be reduced exhaustively to our biological status, to our genetic determinants. What might get lost in such a reductionism would be our openness to transcendence, the call we hear from heaven to transcend our earthly origin. We are a combination of soil and spirit, as Genesis 2:7 reports. Might the reduction of the human reality into a uniform evolutionary biology risk losing the human spirit?

This nervousness has led some theologians to retrieve the ancient doctrine of creationism.[28] According to this view, God creates a new soul for the birth of each human child. This soul is spiritual in its metaphysical makeup. The presence of this soul is what tags the human person as a person and worthy of dignity. In a 1996 elocution, Pope John Paul II affirmed the scientific veracity of the theory of evolution. "Evolution is more than a hypothesis."[29] Yet, when it comes to affirming human dignity, he said that science alone could not account for the presence of the specially created soul. "If the human body takes its origin from the pre-existent living matter, the spiritual soul is immediately created by God."[30] The picture developing here is that we human beings inherit our body from the long history of evolution; but God creates and then imparts a spiritual soul to enliven this body. The body may be the product of evolution, but the soul is not.

Vatican theologians in 2002 reaffirmed the compatibility of biological evolution with the special creation of each spiritual soul. They went further by saying that the human reality—body, soul, and spirit—could be understood in a dynamic fashion, as evolving, as becoming. "In the light of human history and the evolution of human culture, the *imago Dei* can in a real sense be said to be still in the process of becoming."[31]

To assert the special creation of an individual spiritual soul at conception or birth is not the only way Christians can conceive of the soul, to be sure. Other nonmetaphysical understandings of the soul and of the human person are options. We will not delineate them here. However, what is decisive here is that the Christian mind will not be satisfied with reducing the human person exhaustively to his or her biological status, or to a genetic makeup inherited from our evolutionary history. God is calling us to more.

The more to which God calls us includes personal fulfillment, to be sure. It also includes communal unity, as indicated by Jesus' prophecy of the "kingdom of God." In God's kingdom, in contrast to the human kingdoms we have come to know, we will find equality replacing rank and unity replacing division. Such was the yearning of future-looking visionaries at the end of Darwin's century. One late nineteenth-century poet, Henry B. Robins, put it this way:

> Of one blood hath God created
> Every kindred, tribe and tongue;
> He is every fane and altar,
> Though man's empire be far-flung;
> Even though some flout the others,
> Underneath are they blood-brothers;
> And shall learn, some crucial day,
> How to walk a common way.

HUMAN DIGNITY AND ETIL

Just what are the implications of the search for extraterrestrial intelligent life for human dignity? One set of implications has to do with the scientific integrity of SETI; and the other set has to do with speculation about actual contact with ETIL.

As we have said, the Christian faith demands the best science. It is inherent to a faith that seeks understanding that only the most scrupulous and ruthless evaluation of trustworthy evidence count toward human knowledge. However, when it comes to the assumptions made by SETI, we find it difficult to deem this the most scrupulous science. As we have pointed out, the epistemological assumptions proffered by SETI project earth's history of evolution onto earthlike planets in outer space. In addition, SETI adds to Darwin's theory of evolution something that was not there, namely, the origin of life. Darwin could explain the origin of species, not the origin of life. As of this date, no empirical evidence exists that life has originated on a single extraterrestrial planet; nor do we as yet have knowledge of how life begins such that we can even know whether it would fit into the existing theory of evolution. In short, the level of speculation at work among SETI scientists is extreme.

What makes the science of SETI even more suspect is the importation of ideology, specifically the ideology of progress. The doctrine of progress is professed here despite the demurs of some of our more prominent evolutionary biologists, who deny that belief in any guiding principle of design, purpose, or progress constitutes the best science. To carry matters to an even further extreme, some SETI scientists are imagining an extraterrestrial civilization far more advanced than ours, with perfections well beyond ours. Finally, by projecting a functional benevolence onto these extraterrestrial civilizations, they are hoping for help in making earth a better place, a more advanced place. The motivating image for SETI looks like a secularized form of soteriology, a hope that salvation will come from scientists in the sky. SETI looks like a "modern myth of things seen in the sky," to use the phrase Carl Jung applied to UFO belief.

People with faith in God should avoid believing in this scientized myth. If faith demands the best science, then such mythological thinking should become subject to critical scrutiny. Faith in salvation should be placed in God, not in extraterrestrials whom we imagine to have more highly evolved scientific powers.

Despite this demur, we might still ask: suppose what SETI scientists imagine turns out to be true? Suppose their projection of an independent evolutionary history has already occurred on a Goldilocks planet; and suppose ETIL more advanced than us come to visit? Suppose we *Homo sapiens* wake up some day to realize that beings more intelligent than we are governing the interplanetary communications network? What will be the theological implications of extraterrestrial evolution?

Again, let's remind ourselves that the Christian understanding of human dignity is not based on our superiority. It is based on our sharing in the image of God, the *imago Dei*. In the event that we meet ETIL superior to us in some significant fashion, this would not undermine the relationship with God that God has established with us. It would in no way call for us earthlings to deny dignity toward one another. At most, contact with ETIL might add a new race of beings to our dignity list.

Many skeptics wrongfully impute to the Christian vision some sort of investment in human centrality or human superiority. This makes the faith look fragile, ready to collapse with first extraterrestrial contact.[32] This critique reveals a lack of knowledge regarding authentic Christian sensibilities. Friedrich Schleiermacher, for example, writing a couple of decades prior to Darwin in the nineteenth century, celebrated our consciousness of the infinite that transcends us. The religious sense "is the holy wedlock of the Universe with the incarnated Reason for a creative, productive embrace. . . . You lie directly on the bosom of the infinite world. In that moment, you are its soul."[33] Aware of how unfathomable our universe is, we see how small we are in the midst of this infinite. Thus, true religion is oriented by humility. True religion is the sense or feeling of dependence upon something that exceeds us but upon which we depend and are a part. A religious intuition of this sort can combine an open appreciation for the grandeur of our magnificent universe with an appropriate sense of human humility.

In our own era, the founder and director of the Center for Theology and the Natural Sciences in Berkeley, Robert John Russell, supports SETI for theological reasons. He even augments the search for intelligence by suggesting that what is really important is moral agency. We earthlings are moral agents; and we should plan now for moral interaction with ETI. We should be searching for "extraterrestrial intelligent moral agents" or SETMIMA, he argues.[34]

RETRIEVING HUMAN DIGNITY

In summary, despite many claims to the contrary, Charles Darwin's theory that places *Homo sapiens* within the evolution of animals does not undermine the Christian commitment to human dignity. In itself,

Darwin's theory or any other biological theory is unable to provide the philosophical grounding needed to warrant belief in dignity. Affirmation of human worth requires special revelation, special knowledge that our creator deems us so valuable that we are worth redeeming.

Furthermore, faith applies this dignity to each and every human person. A Christian who reads the New Testament cannot help but be impressed with the way that Jesus spent his time with the crippled, the lame, the diseased, the lowly, the poor, and the social outcasts. The very notion of the incarnation—the notion that our sublime God takes on existence as a helpless babe in an animal's manger—reverses the direction of all hierarchies. God dives down to the lower to raise us up higher. This means theologically that no endorsement of an ethic based on the survival of the fittest or a hierarchy of human races can find support in Christian anthropology. The human race is not divided into subspecies ranked on a ladder of lower to higher. Because of the role evolutionary biology has played in justifying some of the most despicable racism and heinous genocides in human history, interpreters of the Darwinian legacy ought not try to find in this science a philosophical warrant for affirming human equality. Science cannot provide the moral ought which we require to treat every person, regardless of race, as equal. What we need to support Darwin's own higher moral sense of universal love is something like trust in a God who declares that all persons, regardless of how low on an alleged evolutionary scale, are equal and worthy of our love.

A Roadmap through Origin of Species

Of course, no anniversary of the publication of Darwin's great work, *On The Origin of Species By Means of Natural Selection, or the Preservation of Favoured Races in the Struggle for Life*, would be complete without a reading of the text. There are many excellent print editions of the work, from the first edition to the definitive sixth edition used by most scholars. For many of us, the look and feel of a book entails a great deal of the pleasure of reading. However, given our digital information age, we have included a CD containing the text of *Origin of Species*, accompanied by a search function that will allow you to quickly locate some of the more interesting ideas in the original. In addition, we would like you to have access to a number of other online resources that may enhance your appreciation of one of the great ideas of our Western scientific culture.

The CD that accompanies this book contains the complete text of the sixth edition of the work, along with a kind of roadmap to its features. We have included a search tool that will allow you to find the location of words or phrases of interest. We've also planned out some specific routes to some of our favorite destinations in the text. Given our common interests in the scientific and theological implications of this work, you'll find that these locations fit the general themes of our commentary. Some of the locations you will tour are:

1. What did Darwin have to say about "design"?
2. What are Darwin's definitions for "natural selection" and "survival of the fittest"?
3. What does Darwin have to say about Herbert Spencer and Thomas Huxley?
4. Where can I find Darwin's support for the notion of progress?
5. What is the definition of "species"? How did Darwin see this as a fluid definition?
6. Did Darwin consider the eye an "irreducibly complex system"?

7. Does Darwin appeal to secondary causation as an explanation?
8. Darwin's rejection of "special creation" in favor of gradual evolution.
9. How did Darwin deal with transitional forms, or missing links, in the chain of evidence?
10. What does Darwin have to say about the nineteenth-century notion that "ontogeny recapitulates phylogeny"?
11. Does Darwin consider the violence inherent in nature to be neutral or wasteful?
12. Darwin's "tangled bank" image of coevolution.

The CD will work with either Windows or Macintosh platforms. Simply insert it into your drive and explore away!

If you'd like to use the Web as a tool for further study, here are some sites of interest that we have found:

1. The Complete Works of Charles Darwin Online (http://darwin-online.org.uk/contents.html). This site contains, of course, all editions of *Origin of Species*, along with much of Darwin's lifelong corpus. The site not only has the text but also details of the publishing history, especially from a bibliophilic perspective.
2. The Darwin Correspondence Project (http://www.darwinproject.ac.uk/index.php). This marvelous site has most of the letters of Charles Darwin. He was a prolific correspondent, and the site includes both letters from and to Darwin. It is searchable and has a subsite entitled "Darwin and Religion" that is quite useful.
3. AboutDarwin.com (http://www.aboutdarwin.com/index.html). This is a site dedicated to Darwin's life and times. It includes new material that receives regular updates regarding events as we approach the anniversaries of Darwin's birth (April) and the publication of *Origin of Species* (November).
4. Charles Darwin's works at Literature.org (http://www.literature.org/authors/darwin-charles/). This site contains the text of four books by Darwin: *The Voyage of the Beagle*, *Origin of Species* (first edition), *Origin of Species* (sixth edition), and *The Descent of Man*.

We know that you will enjoy reading the original text as much as we have.

ANNOTATED BIBLIOGRAPHY

So much has been written about biological evolution, as a science, as a social phenomenon, in support and in opposition. The titles probably number well into the hundreds, just in the last few decades. With this annotated bibliography, we provide a brief set of references for your further study. Admittedly, these represent only a fraction of the available literature. However, they are some of our favorite sources and we hope also represent a cross-section of this field. We have divided this into subtopics using our chapter titles. We have also listed the books in alphabetical order by the author's or first author's last name. In addition, we have appended some comments about each reference, telling you something about the book. You can use this as a guide to explore particular areas of interest that may have been stimulated during your reading.

The Science of Biological Evolution and Related Scientific Concepts (chapters 1 and 4)

Barabási, Albert-László. *Linked: The New Science of Networks.* New York: Perseus Group Books, 2002.
    A readable book by a University of Notre Dame physicist who has been at the forefront of developments in the understanding of scale-free or small-world networks. At present, this field has a major influence on biology.

Campbell, Neil, and Jane Reece. *Biology.* 8th Edition. New York: Benjamin Cummings, 2007.
    There are many basic biology texts available. This one has been used for teaching by Marty and, since he knows it well, we feel comfortable recommending it. This is a source of current information on a number of topics, including evolution, genetics, molecular biology, cell biology, and developmental biology.

Darwin, Charles. *The Origin of Species by Means of Natural Selection,* with an Introduction by Sir Julian Huxley. New York: Signet Classics, 2003.
    This is a reissue of the definitive sixth edition. We have used this text as our source for this book.

Gould, Stephen Jay. *Ontogeny and Phylogeny.* Cambridge, Mass.: Belknap Press of Harvard University Press, 1977.
    Professor Gould, in one of his earliest books, tackled the historical and scientific issues surrounding this supposed comparison. His objective was to free evolutionary biology to allow interaction with developmental biology in the then-new field of evo-devo (evolutionary developmental biology).

———. *The Structure of Evolutionary Theory.* Cambridge, Mass.: Harvard University Press, 2002.
    This is the final work by one of the greatest evolutionary biologists of our age. In this massive volume, Gould explores the science, history, and philosophy of evolutionary biology, with an emphasis on his own positions.

Watts, Duncan. *Six Degrees: The Science of a Connected Age*. New York: W. W. Norton, 2004.
A work by one of the principle contributors to the science of small-world networks. Watts is a professor at Columbia University and at the Santa Fe Institute.

Ideology and Biological Evolution (chapter 2)

Dennett, Daniel C. *Darwin's Dangerous Idea: Evolution and the Meanings of Life*. New York: Simon and Schuster, 1995.
Philosopher Daniel Dennett presents a well-written and cogent defense of evolution, along with his own support for the ideological issues surrounding materialism, reductionism, and atheism.

Hofstadter, Richard. *Social Darwinism in American Thought*. Boston: Beacon Press, 1944, 1992.
This historical tracing of the influence of Herbert Spencer and other social Darwinists on American thought is a classic. All other interpreters rely upon Hofstadter.

Kevles, Daniel J. *In the Name of Eugenics*. Berkeley and Los Angeles: University of California Press, 1985.
This book by a Cal Tech researcher traces the eugenics movement in North America.

Procter, Robert N. *Racial Hygiene: Medicine Under the Nazis*. Cambridge, Mass.: Harvard University Press, 1988.
This disturbing book describes the program of racial hygiene developed in Germany during the period of national socialism, based on the eugenics ideal of improving the human race through speeded-up evolution.

Rose, Hilary, and Steven Rose. *Alas Poor Darwin*. New York: Harmony Books, 2000.
A collection of essays in criticism of sociobiology and evolutionary psychology. Essayists include the Roses, as well as Stephen Jay Gould and Mary Midgley.

Rose, Steven. *Lifelines: Biology Beyond Determinism*. Oxford, England: Oxford University Press, 1997.
Rose critiques the entire program of reductionism in the life sciences from the standpoint of a social rather than a religious position.

Sober, Elliott, and David Sloan Wilson. *Unto Others: The Evolution and Psychology of Unselfish Behavior*. Cambridge, Mass.: Harvard University Press, 1998.
Like naturalistic ethicists in the nineteenth century who sought to ground social theory on biological evolution, sociobiologists and evolutionary psychologists in our own time seek to justify modern liberal ethics on the phenomenon of altruism that seems built into our inherited gene expression. This is a widely respected book on this topic.

Wilson, Edward O. *Consilience: The Unity of Knowledge*. New York: Alfred A. Knopf, 1998.
This Harvard ant researcher gave us the term "sociobiology" with a theory to go along with it: culture is an extension of the gene expression we have inherited from our evolutionary past. All of culture can be explained evolutionarily. By "consilience," Wilson means that all human knowledge can be subsumed under his own discipline, sociobiology.

Wright, Robert. *The Moral Animal*. New York: Pantheon Books, 1994.
This popularization of the fields of sociobiology and evolutionary psychology shows the protean character of these two allegedly scientific extensions of Darwin's biology to psychology and sociology. The book is suggestive, not empirical. Until its theses are confirmed by empirical experi-

ment, we will classify this admittedly fascinating work as a contemporary ideological overlay on top of the Darwinian science.

Theological Issues and Evolution (chapter 3)

His Holiness the Dalai Lama. *The Universe in a Single Atom: The Convergence of Science and Spirituality*. New York: Morgan Road Books, 2005.
The Dalai Lama writes in moving prose about his first encounters with science and his views on science and spirituality. One chapter deals with biological evolution.

Ayala, Francisco J. *Darwin's Gift to Science and Religion*. Washington, DC: Joseph Henry Press, 2007.
Charles Darwin, to the chagrin of his religious contemporaries, expunged design, purpose, and progress from internal biological development. This is a gift to theology, even though theologians might not at first recognize it. It is a gift because theologians can now look for purpose in God rather than nature, which is where they should have been looking all along.

Bowler, Peter J. *Monkey Trials and Gorilla Sermons: Evolution and Christianity from Darwin to Intelligent Design*. Cambridge, Mass.: Harvard University Press, 2007.
This sweep through the nearly two centuries of evolutionary theory shows the subtle and nuanced interactions between the science of Darwinism and both religious objections and accommodations.

Dawkins, Richard. *The Blind Watchmaker*, revised edition. New York: W. W. Norton, 1996.
One of Professor Dawkins's most important works. This contains his arguments in defense of gradualism and reductionism in evolutionary biology.

————. *The God Delusion*. Boston: Houghton Mifflin, 2006.
A long polemic against religion in general and Christianity in particular. Dawkins's position comes out of his conviction that Darwinian evolution necessarily entails atheism.

Deloria, Jr., Vine. *Evolution, Creationism, and Other Modern Myths*. Golden, Colo.: Fulcrum Publishing, 2002.
Another take on evolution issues from one of the most important Native American scholars of our age.

Haught, John, *God After Darwin*. Boulder, Colo.: Westview Press: Perseus Book Group, 2000.
An interesting and important argument for the acceptance of the evolutionary model into Roman Catholic theological reflection. Haught is professor of theology at Georgetown University. This is one of the most influential of recent works in theistic evolution.

Hefner, Philip. *The Human Factor: Evolution, Culture, and Religion*. Minneapolis: Fortress Press, 1993.
After Teilhard, Hefner may provide the most comprehensive integration of evolutionary biology—including sociobiology—with the Christian doctrines of creation and redemption. Evolution has determined that we would be free, writes insightful Hefner. Another example of a book on theistic evolution written by a theologian.

Hoeveler, J. David. *The Evolutionists: American Thinkers Confront Charles Darwin, 1860–1920*. New York: Roman and Littlefield, 2007.
This survey and summary of fourteen major theologians and scientists who have influenced the American mind provides a detailed description of the impact of Darwin's science on social and religious thought.

Miller, Kenneth. *Finding Darwin's God*. New York: Cliff Street Books, 1999.
A critique of intelligent design and related evolution issues from a cell biologist at Brown University. Miller, a scientist, comes down on the side of theistic evolution. Inspiring to scientist readers.

Morris, Henry M. *History of Modern Creationism*. Santee, Calif.: Institute for Creation Research, updated edition, 1993.
This book by the now-late grandfather of scientific creationism not only tells the story of this movement but also provides the essence of its scientific and theological message.

Numbers, Ronald L. *The Creationists: From Scientific Creationism to Intelligent Design*. Cambridge, Mass.: Harvard University Press, expanded edition, 2006.
This is the definitive historical work that describes the development of creationist anti-Darwinism from the nineteenth to twenty-first centuries. Detailed. Enlightening.

Peters, Ted, and Martinez Hewlett. *Evolution: From Creation to New Creation*. Nashville: Abingdon Press, 2003.
This is the first of the books coauthored by Ted and Marty. It provides a detailed summary of the reactions to the Darwinian model: sociobiology, evolutionary psychology, scientific creationism, intelligent design, and theistic evolution. This volume provides more information than the one below, *Can You Believe in God and Evolution?*

————. *Can You Believe in God and Evolution? A Guide for the Perplexed*. Nashville: Abingdon Press, 2006.
We unabashedly recommend our own books because we have studied the books by others and have tried to improve on them. This little book provides in a mere hundred pages a summary of the armies in combat over evolution: the scientists, the materialists, the creationists, the intelligent design advocates, and the theistic evolutionists. This book is less thorough but more readable than the one above, *Evolution: From Creation to New Creation*.

Russell, Robert J. *Cosmology: From Alpha to Omega*. Minneapolis: Fortress Press, 2008.
In this newly released volume, one of the most insightful of today's theistic evolutionists shows how God can act at the level of quantum physics, influencing mutation, yet never breaking a natural law. Divine providence can be made compatible with Darwin's naturalism.

Russell, Robert J., William Stoeger, and Francisco Ayala, editors. *Evolutionary and Molecular Biology: Scientific Perspectives on Divine Action*. Vatican City State: Vatican Observatory Publications, 1998.
A collection of papers from a conference held as part of the Vatican/CTNS series. Although some of the essays are rather technical, there is much to be gained from looking at this book.

Teilhard de Chardin, Pierre. *The Phenomenon of Man*. New York: Harper, 1959.
This Jesuit priest and paleontologist provides the most dramatic and comprehensive version of theistic evolution in the twentieth century. Teilhard is an inspiration to many within both the Christian tradition as well as the new realm of new age spirituality.

Towne, Margaret Gray. *Honest to Genesis: A Biblical and Scientific Challenge to Creationism*. Baltimore: Publish America, 2003.
Towne has written a book directed at fundamentalists who have issues with evolution. She is professor at the University of Las Vegas, Nevada.

Design in Biology and in Theology (chapter 5)

Ayala, Francisco J. *Darwin and Intelligent Design*. Minneapolis: Fortress Press, 2006.
This esteemed former president of the American Association for the Advancement of Science weighs in on the controversy over intelligent design. Although local purpose can be scientifically discerned in the design of the eye, it does not follow that the long history of evolution has been guided by an inner entelechy of progress.

Behe, Michael. *Darwin's Black Box: The Biochemical Challenge to Evolution*. New York: Simon and Schuster, 1996.
One of the two major works by scientists who support intelligent design. Behe provides biological examples of "irreducible complexity," which he argues could not have evolved strictly according to natural selection as Darwin described. Behe is a biochemist at Lehigh University and writes from that scientific perspective.

Dembski, William. *No Free Lunch: Why Specified Complexity Cannot Be Purchased without Intelligence*. Lanham, Md.: Rowman and Littlefield Publishers, Inc., 2001.
One of several books by the other major scientific figure in the intelligent design movement. Dembski approaches this as a theorist from a mathematical and philosophical position.

Johnson, Phillip E. *Darwin on Trial*. Downers Grove, Ill.: InterVarsity Press, 1991.
This book is the shot heard around the world, so to speak. It sounded the beginning of the public debate over intelligent design. By attacking the Darwinian model for its alleged weaknesses, it emboldened the first postcreationist school of thought to develop and consolidate.

Ruse, Michael. *Darwin and Design: Does Evolution Have a Purpose?* Cambridge, Mass.: Harvard University Press, 2003.
An excellent book about design in biology (not about intelligent design), by a philosopher and historian of science.

Scott, Eugenie, and Glenn Branch. *Not In Our Classrooms: Why Intelligent Design Is Wrong for Our Schools*. Boston: Beacon Press, 2006.
A collection of essays attacking the intelligent design movement, produced by the National Center for Science Education.

Evolution and Anthropology (chapter 6)

Bennett, Gaymon, Martinez Hewlett, Ted Peters, and Robert John Russell, editors. *The Evolution of Evil*. Göttingen: Vandenhoeck and Ruprecht, 2008.
This collection of essays addresses the theodicy problem within the evolutionary model: how could a creator God build into the evolutionary process what Darwin called "waste"? That is, why would a benevolent deity construct biology such that predation, extinction, violence, and even genocide are a result of our genetic proclivities? Chapters include contributions from scientists, theologians, historians, and philosophers.

Deacon, Terrence. *The Symbolic Species: The Co-Evolution of Language and the Brain*. New York: W. W. Norton, 1997.
This University of California at Berkeley professor emphasizes the role that the development of language has played in human evolution. His work readies one to perceive the important role that brain development plays in human thought and self-understanding.

Gould, Stephen Jay. *The Mismeasure of Man, revised edition*. New York: W. W. Norton, 1996.
Gould's wonderful historical analysis of the ways in which anthropology has been misused. His book is written as a direct and definitive answer to *The Bell Curve* by Richard J. Herrnstein and Charles Murray, purporting that intelligence has a genetic/racial basis.

Jeeves, Malcolm, editor. *From Cells to Souls: Changing Portraits of Human Nature*. Grand Rapids, Mich.: Eerdemans, 2004.
An informative collection of essays dealing with a variety of views of the human person, from scientific to theological.

Marks, Jonathan. *What It Means to be 98% Chimpanzee: Apes, People, and Their Genes*. Berkeley: University of California Press, 2002.
A provocative book by a molecular anthropologist from the University of North Carolina at Charlotte.

Peters, Ted. *The Evolution of Terrestrial and Extraterrestrial Life*. Goshen Ind.: Pandora Press, 2008.
This brief treatise examines and refutes the claim that Darwinian science must lead to atheism. It takes up the theologian's question of the place of suffering and evil in biological evolution as well as in human morality. It examines the empirical and nonempirical evidence for extraterrestrial life; and it shows what assumptions are made by astrobiologists who look for our own evolutionary future on extrasolar planets.

NOTES

Preface

1. Ted Peters and Martinez Hewlett, *Evolution: From Creation to New Creation* (Nashville: Abingdon Press, 2003); and *Can You Believe in God and Evolution? A Guide for the Perplexed* (Nashville: Abingdon Press, 2006).

2. John Paul II, in *Physics, Philosophy, and Theology*, eds. R. J. Russell, W. R. Stoeger, and G. V. Coyne (Vatican City: Vatican Observatory Foundation, 1997), M13.

1. Origin of Species: *The Science of Darwinian Evolution*

1. Charles Darwin, *On the Origin of Species by Means of Natural Selection* with an Introduction by Sir Julian Huxley, 6th ed. (New York: Signet Classics, 2003), 17.

2. Nora Barlow, *The Autobiography of Charles Darwin 1809–1882, with Original Omissions Restored, Edited with Appendix and Notes by His Grand-Daughter* (London: Collins, 1958), 71.

3. Darwin, *Origin*, 295.

4. Ibid., 76 77.

5. Ibid., 324.

6. Ibid., 75.

7. Ibid., 36.

8. In a cogent though dated article Peter Vorzimmer describes how convinced Darwin was of the idea of blended inheritance. "Charles Darwin and Blending Inheritance" *Isis* 54 (1963): 371–90.

9. Darwin, *Origin*, 28.

10. Ibid., 75.

11. Ibid., 161.

12. Ibid.

13. Ibid.

14. Ibid.

15. St. George Mivart, *The Genesis of Species* (New York: Appleton, 1871). The full text of the book can be found online at http://www.macrodevelopment.org/mivart/Genesis_of_Species.pdf (last accessed 4/13/08).

16. Darwin, *Origin*, 206.

17. Vorzimmer, *Darwin and Blending Inheritance*, 374–77.

18. Fleeming Jenkin, "Review of 'The origin of species.'" *The North British Review* 46 (June 1867): 277–318. The text of the review can be found on the Web at http://www.victorianweb.org/science/science_texts/jenkins.html (last accessed 4/13/08).

19. Vorzimmer, *Darwin and Blending Inheritance*, 387.

20. Jenkin, "Review of 'The origin of species.'"

21. Peter J. Bowler, *Monkey Trials and Gorilla Sermons: Evolution and Christianity from Darwin to Intelligent Design* (Cambridge, Mass.; London: Harvard University Press, 2007), 149.

22. Elizabeth Culotta and Elizabeth Pennisi, "Breakthrough of the Year: Evolution in Action," *Science* 310 (2005): 1878–79.

23. Ibid., 1878.

24. Stephen Jay Gould and Niles Eldredge, "Punctuated equilibria: The tempo and mode of evolution reconsidered," *Paleobiology* 3 (1977): 115–51.

25. Stephen Jay Gould and Richard Lewontin, "The spandrels of San Marco and the Panglossian paradigm: A critique of the adaptationist programme." *Proceedings of the Royal Society London B* 205 (1979): 581–98.

26. Stephen Jay Gould, *The Structure of Evolutionary Theory* (Cambridge, Mass.: Harvard University Press, 2002).

27. Nigel Goldenfeld and Carl Woese, "Biology's next revolution," *Nature* 445 (2007): 369.

2. Drilling through the Layers of Ideology

1. Auguste Comte, *A General View of Positivism*, trans. J. H. Bridges (New York: Speller and Sons, 1957).

2. Francisco Ayala, "Darwin's Devolution: Design without Designer," in *Evolutionary and Molecular Biology: Scientific Perspectives on Divine Action*, eds., R. J. Russell, W. R. Stoeger, and F. J. Ayala (Vatican City: Vatican Observatory and Center for Theology and the Natural Sciences, 1998).

3. Ian G. Barbour, *Issues in Science and Religion* (New York: Harper, 1966) 93–94.

4. Letter from T. H. Huxley to C. Darwin, November 23, 1859, found online at the Darwin Correspondence Project, http://www.darwinproject.ac.uk/darwinletters/calendar/entry-2544.html.

5. The list of the letters and many of the texts are now online at the Darwin Correspondence Project (http://www.darwinproject.ac.uk, last accessed 4/13/08).

6. John Hedley Brooke, *Science and Religion: Some Historical Perspectives* (Cambridge, Mass.: Cambridge University Press, 1991), 41–50.

7. Thomas H. Huxley, "The Coming of Age of the Origin of Species," *Science* 1 (1880): 15–17, 20.

8. Richard Dawkins, *The Blind Watchmaker* (London: W. W. Norton, 1986), 6.

9. Adrian Desmond, *Huxley: Evolution's High Priest* (London: Michael Joseph, 1997).

10. Thomas H. Huxley, *Evolution and Ethics* (Amherst, N.Y.: Prometheus, 1896, 2004), 81–82.

11. Herbert Spencer, *The Data of Ethics* (New York: A. L. Burt Company, 1879) 27–28.

12. Darwin, *Origin*, 75.

13. Spencer did not oppose all forms of aid. Private charity toward the unfit could be approved, but government charity could not.

14. Herbert Spencer, *Social Statics* (New York: D. Appleton & Co., 1864), 414–15.

15. See Jan C. Smuts, *Holism and Evolution* (Cape Town, South Africa: N & S Press, 1925; 1987).

16. Herbert Spencer, *First Principles* (New York: D. Appleton Company, 1897), 407.

17. Ibid., 524.

18. Cited by Richard Hofstadter, *Social Darwinism in American Thought* (Boston: Beacon Press, 1944, 1992), 45.

19. Ibid.

20. John Barrett, "The Problem of the Philippines," *North American Review* CLXVII (1898): 267 in Hofstadter, *Social Darwinism*, 181.

21. Theodore Roosevelt, *The Works of Theodore Roosevelt* (New York: Charles Scribner's Sons, 1926), XIII; 331 in Hofstadter, *Social Darwinism*, 180.

22. For references, see Richard Weikart, "Social Darwinism," *Encyclopedia of Science, Technology, and Ethics*, ed. Carl Mitcham, 4 vols. (New York: Thomson, Gale, 2005) IV:1800–4.

23. Ibid.

24. See chapter 1 of Robert N. Proctor, *Racial Hygiene: Medicine Under the Nazis* (Cambridge, Mass.: Harvard University Press, 1988).

25. Henry M. Morris, *History of Modern Creationism* (Santee, Calif.: Institute for Creation Research, 1993), 50–51.

26. Hofstadter, *Social Darwinism*, 201.

27. Francis Galton, *Memories of My Life* (London: Methuen & Co., 1908), 287 (Web version http://galton.org/books/memories/galton-memories-1up-v2-300dpi.pdf, last accessed 4/13/08).

28. Francis Galton, introduction to *Hereditary Genius: An Inquiry into Its Laws and Consequences* (London: McMillan and Company, 1892). The full text is available at http://www.mugu.com/galton/ (last accessed 4/13/08).

29. The eugenics website can be found at http://www.eugenicsarchive.org/eugenics/ (last accessed 4/13/08).

30. The full text of the opinion can be found at http://www.law.cornell.edu/supct/html/historics/USSC_CR_0274_0200_ZO.html (last accessed 4/13/08).

31. Adolf Hitler, *Mein Kampf*, trans. Ralph Manheim (Boston and New York: Houghton Mifflin Co., 1925, 1971), 285, 287.

32. Joachim C. Fest, *Hitler*, trans. Richard Winston and Clara Winston (New York: Random House Vintage Books, 1975), 208.

33. Darwin, *Origin*, 199.

34. Charles Darwin, *The Autobiography of Charles Darwin*, edited by Nora Barlow (New York: W. W. Norton, 1958) 77.

35. Darwin, *Origin*, 459.

36. Stephen Jay Gould, *Wonderful Life: The Burgess Shale and the Nature of History* (New York: W. W. Norton, 1989).

3. The Many Theologies of Evolution

1. Charles Darwin, *On the Origin of Species by Means of Natural Selection* with an Introduction by Sir Julian Huxley, 6th ed. (New York: Signet Classics, 2003).

2. Ibid.

3. Charles Darwin, *The Life and Letters of Charles Darwin, Including an Autobiographical Chapter*, ed. Francis Darwin, 3 vols. (London: John Murray, 1888), 2:311.

4. Michael Ruse, "Darwinism: Foe or Friend?" *The Evolution of Rationality: Interdisciplinary Essays in Honor of J. Wentzel van Huyssteen*, ed. F. LeFron Shults (Grand Rapids, Mich.: Eerdmans, 2006), 231.

5. Thomas Huxley, *Evolution and Ethics* (Amherst, N.Y.: Prometheus, 1896, 2004), 71.

6. Answers in Genesis, http://www.answersingenesis.org/. For a comprehensive exposition and analysis of creationism, see Ronald L. Numbers, *The Creationists: From Scientific Creationism to Intelligent Design*, expanded edition (Cambridge, Mass.: Harvard University Press, 2006) and chapter 4 of Ted Peters and Martinez Hewlett, *Evolution: From Creation to New Creation* (Nashville: Abingdon Press, 2003).

7. Institute for Creation Research, http://www.icr.org/ (last accessed 4/13/08).

8. Darwin, *Origin*, 443.

9. Ibid., 158.

10. Ibid., 166.

11. Frank J. Poelwijk, Daniel J. Kiviet, Daniel M. Weinreich, and Sanders J. Tans, "Empirical Fitness Landscapes Reveal Accessible Evolutionary Paths," *Nature* 445 (2007): 383–86.

12. Henry M. Morris, *History of Modern Creationism*, 2nd ed. (El Cajon, Calif.: Institute for Creation Research, 1993), 297.

13. Henry M. Morris, *Scientific Creationism* (Green Forest, Ark.: Master Books, 1974; 1985), 219.

14. Ibid., 228.

15. For basic texts by intelligent design advocates see: Phillip E. Johnson, *Darwin on Trial* (Washington, DC: Regnery Gateway, 1991); Michael Behe, *Darwin's Black Box: The Biochemical Challenge to Evolution* (New York: Touchstone/Simon and Schuster, 1996); and William Dembski, *No Free Lunch: Why Specified Complexity Cannot Be Purchased without Intelligence* (New York and Plymouth, England: Rowman and Littlefield, 2002). For a critical review of Intelligent Design, see chapter 17 of Numbers, *The Creationists*; chapter 5 of Peters and Hewlett, *Evolution*; Francisco Ayala, *Darwin and Intelligent Design* (Minneapolis: Fortress Press, 2006); and *Not in Our Classrooms: Why Intelligent Design Is Wrong for Our Schools*, ed. Eugenie C. Scott and Glenn Branch (Boston: Beacon Press, 2006).

16. Darwin, *Origin*, 175.

17. Among the Turkish Muslim voices raised in opposition to Darwinian evolution, that of Harun Yahya is the loudest. See his book *The Evolution Deceit: The Scientific Collapse of Darwinism and Its Ideological Background* (Istanbul: Okur Publishing, 2000) and website: www.hyahya.org (last accessed 4/13/08).

18. Peter J. Bowler, *Monkey Trials and Gorilla Sermons: Evolution and Christianity from Darwin to Intelligent Design* (Cambridge, Mass.; London: Harvard University Press, 2007), 81.

19. See chapter 4 of J. David Hoeveler, *The Evolutionists: American Thinkers Confront Charles Darwin, 1860–1920* (New York: Rowman and Littlefield, 2007); and B. B. Warfield, *Evolution, Scripture, and Science*, eds. Mark A. Noll and Daniel N. Livingstone (Grand Rapids, Mich.: Baker Books, 2000).

20. Pierre Teilhard de Chardin, *The Phenomenon of Man* (New York: Harper, 1959), 146.

21. Ibid., 294.

22. Bowler, *Monkey Trials and Gorilla Sermons*, 28–29.

23. Robert John Russell, "Does the 'God Who Acts' Really Act in Nature?" *Science and Theology: The New Consonance*, ed. Ted Peters (Boulder, Colo.: Westview, 1998), 79; italics in original.

24. Edward K. Wagner, Martinez J. Hewlett, David Bloom, and David Camerini, *Basic Virology*, 3rd ed. (Oxford, England: Blackwell, 2007).

4. Scientific Concepts: Then and Now

1. See, for instance, a recent textbook on evolutionary biology, S. Freeman and H. Herron, *Evolutionary Analysis*, 3rd ed. (Upper Saddle River, N.J.: Prentice Hall, 2004). The species concepts are treated on pages 584–87.

2. Charles Darwin, *On the Origin of Species by Means of Natural Selection* with an Introduction by Sir Julian Huxley, 6th ed. (New York: Signet Classics, 2003), 65.

3. Ernst Mayr, "Darwin's Principle of Divergence," *Journal of the History of Biology* 25 (1992): 343–59.

4. Ernst Mayr, "What Is a Species, and What Is Not?" *Philosophy of Science* 63 (1996): 262–77.

5. Freeman and Herron, *Evolutionary Analysis*, 584.

6. Nigel Goldenfeld and Carl Woese, "Biology's Next Revolution," *Nature* 445 (2007): 369.

7. Mayr, "What Is a Species," 262–77.

8. The complete collection of these reports can be found online at http://darwin-online.org.uk/ (last accessed 4/13/08).

9. Freeman and Herron, *Evolutionary Analysis*, 48.

10. Francesca D. Ciccarelli, Tobias Doerks, Christian von Mering, Christopher J. Creevey, Berend Snel, and Peer Bork, "Toward Automatic Reconstruction of a Highly Resolved Tree of Life," *Science* 311 (2006): 1283–87.

11. The site is located at http://www.ornl.gov/sci/techresources/Human_Genome/project/timeline.shtml (last accessed 4/13/08).

12. J. Craig Venter et al., "The Sequence of the Human Genome," *Science* 291 (2001): 1304–51.

13. An excellent commentary on this state of affairs has been published by one of the giants of modern biology, Carl Woese, "A New Biology for a New Century," *Microbiology and Molecular Biology Reviews* 68 (2004): 173–86.

14. Darwin, *Origin*, 158.

15. The International HapMap Consortium (literally hundreds of researchers), "A Haplotype Map of the Human Genome," *Nature* 437 (2005): 1299–1320. One year earlier, the Consortium authored an opinion piece in the journal *Nature* that was a defense of their methodology and the expected benefits to be obtained. That opinion paper is "Integrating Ethics and Science in the Human HapMap Project," *Nature Reviews: Genetics* 5 (2004): 467–75.

16. Troy Duster, "Race and Reification in Science," *Science* 307 (2005): 1050–51.

17. Charlotte Hunt-Grubbe, "The Elementary DNA of Dr. Watson," The Sunday Times, October 14, 2007, found online at http://entertainment.timesonline.co.uk/tol/arts_and_entertainment/books/article2630748.ece (last accessed 4/13/08).

18. Darwin, *Origin*, 76.

19. Ibid., 444.

20. Quoted from an American edition of Herbert Spencer's 1861 book, *Principles of Biology*, vol. 1 (New York: D. Appleton and Company, 1902), 530–31.

21. Darwin, *Origin*, 75.

22. Alfred, Lord Tennyson, *In Memoriam A.H.H.*, Canto LVI, found at http://www.theotherpages.org/poems/books/tennyson/tennyson04.html (last accessed 4/13/08).

23. This is the well-known story that documents the darkening of tree trunks due to industrial activity, and the concomitant increase in Melanic (darker) variants of the moth, due to predation by birds of the more easily visible lighter variants. With the reversal of the effects of pollution, this situation changed back to the original. Although the work has been wrongly criticized by antievolution writers, the observations have been verified recently. See *Science* 317 (2007): 1301.

24. Darwin, *Origin*, 419.

25. Ibid

26. Sigmund Freud, *Totem and Taboo: Some Points of Agreement between the Mental Lives of Savages and Neurotics*, trans. James Strachey (New York: W. W. Norton, 1950), 1. Our thanks to Kathy Armistead for this point.

27. Michael K. Richardson, et al., "There Is No Highly Conserved Embryonic Stage in the Vertebrates: Implications for Current Theories of Evolution and Development," *Anatomical Embryology* 196 (1997): 91–106.

28. Stephen Jay Gould, *Ontogeny and Phylogeny* (Cambridge, Mass.: Belknap Press of Harvard University Press, 1977).

29. The website in question is "The Talk Origins Archive." The page in question related to dating of the earth is located at http://www.talkorigins.org/faqs/faq-age-of-earth.html.

30. The terms *paradigm* and *paradigm shift* were introduced by Thomas Kuhn in his book, *The Structure of Scientific Revolutions* (Chicago: University of Chicago Press, 1962).

31. The International Human Genome Consortium (hundreds of authors), "Finishing the Achromatic Sequence of the Human Genome," *Nature* 431 (2004): 931–45.

32. Michael Snyder and Mark Gerstein, "Defining Genes in the Genomics Era," *Science* 300 (2003): 258–60.

33. Two recent books that cover aspects of scale-free networks are Albert-László Barabási, *Linked: The New Science of Networks* (Cambridge, Mass.: Perseus Books Group, 2002) and Duncan Watts, *Six Degrees: The Science of a Connected Age* (New York: W. W. Norton, 2004).

34. Examples of interactomes in the recent literature include: L. Gigot, et al., "A Protein Interaction Map of *Drosophila melanogaster*," *Science* 302 (2003): 1727–36; S. Li, et al., "A Map of the Interactome Network of the Metazoan C. *elegans*," *Science* 303 (2004): 540–43.

5. Design in Biology: What Darwin Could and Could Not See

1. Michael Ruse, *Darwin and Design: Does Evolution Have a Purpose?* (Cambridge, Mass.: Harvard University Press, 2003). Reviewed by Martinez Hewlett, *Theology and Science*, 1 (2004), 151-53.

2. Charles Darwin, *On the Origin of Species by Means of Natural Selection* with an Introduction by Sir Julian Huxley, 6th ed. (New York: Signet Classics, 2003), 453.

3. Ibid., 111.

4. Ibid., 459.

5. William Paley, *Natural Theology, Or Evidences of the Existence and Attributes of the Deity*, eds. M. Eddy and D. Knight (Oxford, England: Oxford University Press, 2006).

6. Richard Dawkins's *The Blind Watchmaker* (New York: W. W. Norton, 1986) takes its title as a slam against the Paley view.

7. Thomas Aquinas, *Summa Theologica*, Q. 2, Art. 3 (Chicago: *Encyclopedia Britannica*, 1952), 13.

8. Both Richard Dawkins and William Dembski make these mistakes in their writings. Dembski proposes something he calls "intelligent causes" without clarifying what he means by this in accurate philosophical terms (see *No Free Lunch* [Lanham, Md.: Rowman & Littlefield, 2002], xiii). Dawkins, for his part, totally confuses Thomas Aquinas's arguments and conflates the "design argument" with the Fifth Way (see *The God Delusion* [Boston: Houghton Miflin, 2006], 77–79).

9. A number of recent writers have espoused the theistic evolution perspective. For instance, cell biologist Ken Miller, *Finding Darwin's God* (New York: Cliff Street Books, 1999), and theologian John Haught, *God after Darwin* (Boulder, Colo.: Westview Press, 2000), both argue from this position. And, of course, the authors of this book have produced their own entries in this field; see Peters and Hewlett, *Evolution: From Creation to New Creation* (Nashville: Abingdon Press, 2003), and *Can You Believe in God and Evolution? A Guide for the Perplexed* (Nashville: Abingdon Press, 2006).

10. Letter from Charles Darwin to Asa Gray, dated May 22, 1860, found at the Darwin Correspondence Project website (http://www.darwinproject.ac.uk/darwinletters/calendar/entry-2814.html, last accessed 4/13/08).

11. These terms are defined in the key works by these two authors. See, for instance, Michael Behe in *Darwin's Black Box* (New York: Touchstone, 1996) and William Dembski in *No Free Lunch* (Lanham, Md.: Rowman & Littlefield, 2002).

12. These kinds of evolutionary changes are reviewed by Lynn Margulis in *Symbiosis as a Source of Evolutionary Innovation: Speciation and Morphogenesis*, eds., L. Margulis and R. Fester (Cambridge: MIT Press, 1991), 1–14.

13. Stephen Jay Gould's final masterpiece is a tome worthy of anyone's library. *The Structure of Evolutionary Theory* (Cambridge, Mass.: Harvard University Press, 2002) is a book in which Gould addresses everything from the history of Darwin and his work to Gould's own groundbreaking ideas.

14. Nigel Goldenfeld and Carl Woese, "Biology's Next Revolution," *Nature* 445 (2007): 369.

6. What Does It Mean to Be Human?

1. "Introduction by Sir Julian Huxley" in *On the Origin of Species by Natural Selection*, by Charles Darwin, 6th ed. (New York: Signet Classics, 2003), 16.

2. Sigmund Freud, *Introductory Lectures on Psycho-Analysis*, trans. and ed. James Strachey (New York: W. W. Norton, 1966), 353.

3. John Hedley Brooke, *Science and Religion: Some Historical Perspectives* (Cambridge, Mass.: Cambridge University Press, 1991).

4. Darwin, *Origin*, 345. As we pointed out earlier, Darwin and today's Darwinians are ambivalent on the concept of progress. On the one hand, Darwin can say that "natural selection, or the survival

of the fittest, does not necessarily include progressive development"(125). On the other hand, natural selection always works for the betterment of the species; and, in addition, it leads to increased complexity of structure and increased intelligence. Darwin clearly thought this to be an advance.

5. Charles Darwin, *Descent of Man*, chapter 3, "Comparison of the Mental Powers of Man and the Lower Animals—Continued," in *From So Simple a Beginning: The Four Great Books of Charles Darwin*, ed. Edward O. Wilson (New York: W. W. Norton, 2006), 837.

6. Darwin, *Descent of Man*, 908–9.

7. Ibid., 836.

8. Herbert Spencer, *The Data of Ethics* (New York: A. L. Burt Co., 1879), 28–29.

9. Darwin, *Descent of Man*, 815.

10. Ibid.

11. Ibid., 816.

12. Ibid.

13. Ibid.

14. Darwin, *Origin*, 452.

15. Edna Devore, "Voyages Through Time," *SETI Institute News*, 12:1 (First Quarter 2003): 7.

16. Christian de Duve, *Vital Dust: The Origin and Evolution of Life on Earth* (New York: Basic Books, 1995), xv.

17. Cited by Diane Richards, "Interview with Dr. Frank Drake," *SETI Institute News*, 12:1 (First Quarter 2003): 5.

18. Paul Davies, *Are We Alone? Implications of the Discovery of Extraterrestrial Life?* (New York: Penguin, 1995), 32–33.

19. Ibid., 33.

20. Jill Cornell Tarter, "SETI and the Religions of the Universe," *Many Worlds: The New Universe, Extraterrestrial Life and the Theological Implications*, ed. Steven Dick (Philadelphia and London: Templeton Foundation Press, 2000), 146.

21. Carl Sagan, *Pale Blue Dot: A Vision of the Human Future in Space* (New York: Random House, 1994), 33.

22. Francisco J. Ayala, "The Evolution of Life on Earth and the Uniqueness of Humankind," *Perché esiste qualcosa invece di nulla? (Why Is There Something Rather than Nothing?)* eds. S. Moriggi and E. Sindoni (Castel Bolognese, Italy: ITACAlibri, 2004), 57–77.

23. Darwin, *Origin*, 244–46.

24. Vatican: International Theological Commission, *Communion and Stewardship: Human Persons Created in the Image of God* 2002 (25), http://www.vatican.ca/roman_curia/congregations/cfaith/cti_documents/rc_con_cfaith_doc (last accessed 4/13/08).

25. Joshua Moritz, "Natures, Human Nature, Genes and Souls? Reclaiming Theological Anthropology Through Biological Structuralism," *Dialog* 46:3 (Fall 2007), 277.

26. Richard Wrangham and Dale Peterson, *Demonic Males: Apes and the Origins of Human Violence* (Boston and New York: Houghton Mifflin, Mariner Books, 1996), 198. The difference between human DNA and chimp DNA is only 1.23 percent. See: Michael D. Lemonick and Andrea Dorfman, "What Makes Us Different?" *Time* 168:15 (October 9, 2006): 44–53.

27. Vatican, *Communion and Stewardship*, 46.

28. The term *creationism* has two overlapping meanings. On the one hand, as we saw in an earlier chapter, it refers to a school of theological thought that repudiates Darwinian evolution and substitutes the belief that God creates each kind or species independently. On the other hand, the Vatican uses the term to refer to the special creation of each person's soul. The latter use of *creationism* is compatible with evolutionary biology, whereas the former is not.

29. Pope John Paul II, "Evolution and the Living God," *Science and Theology: The New Consonance*, ed. Ted Peters (Boulder, Colo.: Westview Press, 1998), 150.

30. Ibid., 151.

31. Vatican, *Communion and Stewardship*, 24.

32. For example, see Paul Davies, *God and the New Physics* (New York: Simon and Schuster, 1983), 71.

33. Friedrich Schleiermacher, *On Religion: Speeches to Its Cultured Despisers*, trans. Rudolf Otto (New York: Harper and Bros., 1799, 1958), 43.

34. Robert John Russell, "Five Key Topics on the Frontier of Theology and Science Today," *Dialog* 46:3 (Fall 2007): 205.